How do you carry a c[...]
easy! Slip it into a jean or jacket pocket, in
a knapsack, in a glove compartment, in a
bedroll, in a plastic cup, or in a shoe.

This special cookbook is written just for:
- camp counselors, outtripping howling youngsters bent on a delicious hamburger treat
- college kids hunting menus for a special
  campout
- Mom, family camp chef, who wants something simple
- canoeists, outward bound and always hungry
- teen church groups off on a wingding picnic
  in the woods.

Warm, happy memories of stick-roasting crispy
Pioneer Drumsticks over hot coals; of Doughboys, hot and puffy, loaded with butter and
jelly; of sweet Somemores, a chocolate
marshmallow treat, and oh-so-many-more
goodies are recorded here for you.

These recipes and menus, kept simple, can
guide you into a memorable adventure in
campfire cooking.

CAMPFIRE COOKING

Yvonne Messner

David C. Cook Publishing Co.
850 NORTH GROVE AVENUE • ELGIN, IL 60120
In Canada: David C. Cook Publishing (Canada) Ltd., Weston, Ontario M9L 1T4

David C. Cook Publishing Co., Elgin, IL 60120

Printed in the United States of America
Library of Congress Catalog Number: 73-90003
ISBN: 0-912692-29-4

To my dearest Dick, Mick,
Merilyn, and Lovey
and
other campers who love to eat

CONTENTS

Preface

We are running away from the home kitchen as never before. This book suggests that rather than running to the fast-food places, why not try an exciting adventure cooking in the out-of-doors?

Even when we eat "in," we are "eating out" more and more. The foods we eat have increasing amounts of built-in chef service. More than half the food we buy is ready to cook, reports the Department of Agriculture, and most of the rest is ready to eat. Only three percent needs further preparation. Far from the humdrum kitchen routine with a thousand and one gadgets, campfire cooking takes much less time, with hardly a handful of tools.

Nearly all your favorite foods can be fixed outdoors when you know how. Take your favorite cut of meat, put it on a grill over a hot bed of coals. The lick of the flames will give it that distinct charcoal flavor. Mix with tender, tasty vegetables, a crisp, tossed salad and the subtle seasoning of sun and pine-scented breezes. Result: One delicious, delightful meal.

With the restlessness of people today and young people in particular, and the increasing desire to "be on the move," it makes sense to eat in the out-of-doors. Food always tastes better outdoors.

Nothing can match the memorable experiences of cooking around the campfire; of seeing hungry campers readily devour all in sight. And long after the meal, of sharing times around the fire. And then, with powdery coals fading, a late night snack.

Anyone who says he's "roughing it" when he cooks outdoors probably doesn't know the basic camping skills. This book is designed to make you the best camp cook around. From the neophyte to the most experienced camper, I'm sure you'll find ideas galore to make camp mealtime simple and very special.

YVONNE MESSNER

Planning Meals Out

When you plan a camping trip anywhere, you have three big responsibilities. First, planning a nutritious menu and deciding what food to take. Second, accounting for the numbers of hungry mouths and hardy appetites, and deciding how much food to take. Finally, deciding how to get it all together. This means packing, refrigerating, and conserving everything possible. Long-trip planners must make extra consideration of total weight allowed, water supply available, protection from animals, and numerous other things.

Food to Take

First, figure up exactly how many meals you need to pack for. Sit down and write out tentative menus for the number of breakfasts you must fix. Do the same for lunches and dinners. Try to vary them each day. Write out some snack items for after big hikes or late at night before bedtime. Remember to include the four food groups to make the meals as nutritious as possible.

Once you have the menu, write out next to each item in the menu the specific ingredients needed for the amount of people you must feed. As a camp counselor, camp director, and mother I've had to do this many times.

It should look something like this:

Menu	Market List
Breakfast for 5	5 oranges
Fresh oranges, quartered	2 cups pancake mix
Pancakes, butter, syrup	1¼ c. milk + 3 c. milk
Bacon	(kids)
Milk, coffee (black)	½ lb. bacon
	1 stick margarine
	1 c. syrup
	2 tsp. instant coffee

For additional menu ideas and market lists see the section on Trip Counselor's Menus.

After you have made out menus and market lists for each day, make a composite list of all the items you need. Divide them into such categories as fruits, vegetables, meats, mixes, drinks, desserts, snacks, etc. Then you are ready to buy the items. Trip counselors: food and utensils can usually be obtained from the camp kitchen and camp cook.

Before you buy, go over your list carefully to see where you can make adjustments in your menus to avoid buying excess items. For instance, if you need 18 oranges and they come 12 to a bag, then change a snack item to include oranges, or delete 6 oranges and substitute a powdered can of juice (quart size) for breakfast instead. You'll be surprised how much you can cut down this way.

Don't overlook freeze-dried items in your meal planning. On page 41 is a list of lightweight foods available at your grocers.

If you're backpacking, see the section on Trail Travelers; most of your foods should be dehydrated or freeze-dried.

If you're going to be in the city, or near stores, you

really don't have to worry. But remember, when you don't plan ahead, you spend more.

If you are to be in an area where fresh fruits are wild and plentiful, plan these in your menus; they will be delicious and save you money as well.

On one camping trip we didn't have refrigeration for frozen items, so we had to eliminate ice cream (a family favorite). And we didn't stock frozen French fries or even a lot of potato chips. Guess what. We all lost about five pounds without knowing it, and were we ever happy!

Don't leave out salt, pepper, catsup, mustard, relish, syrup, jelly, and the like. Once some girls planned a big hot dog picnic supper for some hikers for an organization I sponsored and I thought they could make out the menu and get everything themselves. But when we prepared to leave I discovered their total supplies included hot dogs, a cake, and a pot of lemonade. No buns, no relish, no cake server, no ladle, no cups, and no napkins. Then I realized that all planning groups, no matter what age, need a little guidance in meal planning. That brings us to the next item.

Utensils to Take

Start out with the first breakfast menu and begin to list all the utensils needed. Bring only the minimum. Utensils add weight to a trip vehicle. Remember, some items can be made from heavy foil (See Handmade Cooking Utensils, Tin Can, and Aluminum Foil Cookery).

Bring only one set of plates and silverware for each. It's easier to wash them than to carry the extra load. Some campers have their own mess kits.

Things like paper towels, dishcloths, hot pads, dish towels, dishwashing liquid, and scratchers are most often forgotten because they are not food items. Also throw in some clothesline and a few pins. Dishcloths and towels sometimes take forever to dry in humid areas. Hang them on a line in the sunshine or in the tent if need be. To keep towels from getting black, rub off the black soot from the bottoms of pots and pans with paper towels

13

before washing. If you soap the pan's bottom before placing it on the fire the black should come off easily.

See the section on Basic Cooking Utensils before you complete your list.

Packing Food and Utensils

The backpacker has only so much room which dictates what must be left home. The canoeist must pack things compactly and securely to place under the thwarts of his boat. But the average camper has a car trunk or trip vehicle to carry supplies. Some guidelines might be helpful:

1. Put aside meal items to be used first on the trip.

2. Decide on how much refrigeration will be needed for such perishable items as meats and fresh vegetables. Secure a cooler large enough for your needs.

3. Remember: bacon, cheese, peanut butter, jelly, catsup and mustard do not need refrigeration. You do it at home for convenience. (Bacon in slab is best, wrapped in vinegar cloth.)

4. Separate all glass and paper containers, transfer to plastic containers if possible. Tupperware is great for this.

5. Put cardboard boxes to one side (include containers of cold and hot cereals). Transfer to plastic containers or plastic bags. Keep instructions within plastic.

6. If using cardboard boxes for carrying, select those with low sides and firm bottoms.

7. Put eggs in flour to transport. Use salt and pepper supplies for shakers as well.

8. Nest all bowls, cups, and dishes for compactness.

9. Use utensils for more than one purpose. One large pot can be a skillet, a saucepan, a cooker, a Dutch oven, and an oven (see biscuit baking under One-Pot Meals).

10. Large vacuum bottles come in handy for keeping eggs (just break one at a time into bottle) or they can keep your first day's lunch hot. Mix a stew and store it in a vacuum bottle until ready to use. Keep hot water

in a bottle for hot drinks along the road or when you first arrive; summer, cool drinks. Buy a good vacuum bottle for best results.

11. If you must carry all your water, the best is a five-gallon container with a pouring spout at the bottom. They now come in sturdy lightweight plastic.

12. Buy all *fresh* meat and produce to last longer. Freeze all meat before leaving; it will defrost by the time you need it.

Safe Refrigeration

It's possible to get along without a camp stove, but one thing you can't do without is proper refrigeration.

Backpackers and wilderness campers must let dehydrated foods do or make a spring box (Fig. 12). But most campers take along some type of cooler. If you're carrying such perishables as fresh meat, milk and butter, a cooler is imperative.

Coolers come in all shapes and sizes. A metal one with good insulation (such as urethane) is better than the inexpensive foam cooler which breaks easily.

Some other things to look for in a cooler are: Large enough to hold a block of ice; shelf to put small items on; inside corners rounded for easy cleaning; door or lids seal tightly; adequate drainage system; handles fixed for easy carrying; stainproof and rustproof interior.

Buy it big enough. An 11 gallon box is about right for weekend trips. You will have to pay around $25.

Remember these facts from the U.S. Public Health Service:

Products high in protein and moisture such as milk, milk products, eggs, meat, poultry, fish, cream pies, custards, potato salad and the like, are fast producers of disease bacteria.

If you do not have the facilities for maintaining these foods hot or cold, do not take them!

Do not refrigerate in deep containers. Food acts as an insulator and the center of large masses can be warm for long periods of time even though the outer edges may be almost frozen. Use shallow pans and fill no more than three to four inches deep.

Remember, refrigeration does not kill disease-producing bacteria. It only slows their growth.

Cover the serving area (ground, blanket or table) with a tablecloth to provide a clean surface on which to place food. Food should be kept covered except when being prepared or served.

Return leftover potentially hazardous food to the ice chest immediately after the meal. If there is no ice left, or the food has been left at an unsafe temperature, *throw it out*. The best plan is to limit food quantities to avoid leftovers. Don't make the mistake of serving foods at lunchtime, then leaving them unrefrigerated to be served again later in the day.

Several days before you plan to go camping, you may want to freeze your own ice in quart or half-gallon milk containers. A good idea is to freeze fruit juices in plastic containers and use them as they thaw. A block of ice is superior to ice cubes which melt fast. If you do use cubes, keep them in a plastic container, don't scatter them around. Take out cold items quickly and replace the lid immediately to conserve the cold. Chill all foods, including fruits and vegetables, the night before, so they will be cold when they go into the box.

When you arrive at camp, store the cooler in a cool, shady place. Throw a tarp over it for extra insulation, and be sure to drain off any melted ice water.

Finally, if you keep perishables more than two days in a hot climate, you will have to put in a new block of ice. Discard the small chunk that's left. It isn't doing the job.

Safe Storage

If you've been camping at all, you no doubt have seen what raccoons do at night to garbage cans or any food they find. They maul it, paw it, devour it, and leave a big mess. So be careful where you store your food when darkness falls.

Your perishables will be in your tightly closed cooler or encased in a well of stones in the cool water or in a spring box. Many other food items are left to be cared for—bread, cereal, packaged mixes, syrup, sugar, salt, pepper, other condiments and staples.

Many trip campers have traveled in cars and can put these items in the trunk. While others who have come by foot, bike, canoe, or horseback will have a problem —unless you make a *cache* to keep food off the ground and away from animals.

There are many different kinds of caches you can make. One is to bend a small green sapling over, attach the food to the end of the branch, then let it fly back into place. This is great for protection from large animals, but may be a feast for the ants unless it is well protected in tightly sealed plastic.

Another cache is called the "peeled-stick" cache (Fig. 13). Peel a large stick, place in the crotches of two trees (use a forked stick to lift it up). Then throw a rope over it, tie on the bag of food, pull up high, tie other end around one of the trees with a couple of half hitches. The slippery peeled stick keeps animals from having a good footing to get to the food.

If you don't want to take the time to peel a stick, just throw the rope over a limb, cut a hole in an empty tin can, slide it up the rope, then tie on the food, pull up, and tie to the tree. The tin can discourages ants from coming down to the food, and also makes noise if a small crawling animal should try to reach the food (See Fig. 13).

Anything with a salty taste has a fatal attraction for bugs. Perspiration-soaked paddles, axes, shoes, belts, bridles, and saddles must be kept well out of their reach. If you're in an area where the marauders might be bears, wolves, or porcupines, and there is a possibility of them biting through cans, better cache these items too.

To keep the ever-present flies, ants, and other tiny bugs that love to sample food and get in your hair from

17

crawling up the table, put the legs in cans of water. A few mothballs or moth flakes around the table legs will also help keep ants away. For flying insects, keep lids tight on food in containers on the table. Remove covers only for serving. Other items may be wrapped in waxed paper or cheesecloth. Use insect spray just before meals to keep most flies away.

Safe Water

Survival manuals tell us that even in cold areas the human body needs two quarts of water a day to maintain efficiency. Of course some of it can be provided by food and other beverages. But we also know that in hot weather or following strenuous activity, much more water may be required.

Wherever you go to camp, you should know that there will be good water waiting for you, or else you must take it with you.

Most commercial campgrounds and many public campgrounds have drinking water available. But when checking the water be sure it is meant for those purposes. If not, purify the water by boiling it for a minimum of five minutes or by adding three drops (six drops if water is cloudy) of two percent tincture of iodine per quart of water and let it stand for one hour; or by using water purification tablets according to directions on the package. Water from melted snow should be purified in the same way as any other questionable water. Add a little salt to boiled water to make it palatable. Tea also makes it more pleasant to taste.

Wilderness sites may have a cold stream or lake or a spring from which you can get water. Chances are, if it's far from civilized man, it will be clean and pure. But you can't be sure. Appearance isn't always a true test. So it pays to purify it.

Preservative Equipment

Plastic containers and tubes, all sizes
Plastic bags

Camp cooker or spring box (ice pick)
Vacuum jugs
Water containers
Purification tablets, iodine
Rope for hanging caches

Basic Cooking Tools and Utensils

Having the right equipment along on a camping venture means peace of mind. It's annoying to carry things you don't need. On the other hand, to be without an important tool or utensil is frustrating. Listed below are items that you absolutely need to do the job.

Preparing the Stove

Sharp ax to split wood
Folding camp shovel
Bucket for watering unwanted sparks
Handsaw for cutting wood pieces
Grate (or grid) large enough for stove top
Kitchen type matches in waterproof case

Preparing the Meal

Good-sized, long-handled, hinged grill
Cast-iron skillet or two
Large heavy pot with handle
Heavy pans with lids
Old coffeepot or old kettle
Kitchen knives
Long-handled spoon, fork, spatula, and ladle
Can and bottle openers
Hot pads, cooking mitt
Heavy-duty aluminum foil
Tupperware mixing and storage bowls

Family campers may want to take old pots and pans

from home rather than buy them new from camping outfitters. Nest pans together with bowls and pack them for a short trip to try them out before leaving on that long vacation.

Serving the Meal

The number of plates, cups and sets of silverware will vary according to the size of your group. It is best to take light plastic plates, cups, and glasses. Paper items are all right for short trips, but for ecology's sake, it is better to wash your dishes. If you have to take paper, make it white. It's easier dissolved.

The following utensils are basic serving items:

1 plate per person
1 cup each for hot drinks, soups, desserts
1 glass each for cold drinks, juices, sodas
1 fork, knife, spoon, per person
Serving spoons
Serving bowls
Serving platters
Sugar bowl, preferably covered as in Tupperware.
Salt and pepper shakers, also with covered tops.
Tablecloth, napkins, paper towels
Regular dessert dishes
Large soup or cereal bowls are optional.

If space is a factor, mixing bowls can be used to serve food in.

Cleaning Up

Figure on enough pots for boiling water for both washing and rinsing the dishes. Soap left on dishes may cause diarrhea. As we mentioned earlier, always soap well the bottom of all pots and pans before cooking over your outdoor stove. Also, it will make dishwashing a lot easier if, immediately after eating, you use paper towels to wipe dishes, silverware, pots, and pans as clean of food as possible. Be sure to bring along some soap-filled scouring pads. They really finish the job. Wadded up pieces of used aluminum foil make good scratchers. Toss used paper towels in the fire or put in refuse receptacle, along with the garbage. If no receptacle is available, dig a hole and bury the garbage. Leftover dishwater should not be thrown on the grass or sloshed on the ground. It attracts insects. Best place for it is on the fire. There never seem to be enough dishcloths and dish towels because they often don't dry in time for the next meal, so take plenty. Old hand towels can serve a double purpose—for dirty kids and dirty dishes.

Clean-Up Items

Plastic bags, film wrap, waxed paper
Plastic garbage bags
Soap-filled scouring pads
Sponges
Plastic dishpan
Dishwashing detergent (plastic bottle)
Dishcloths, dish towels
Camp broom
Folding camp shovel

Handmade Cooking Tools

If at camp you need some tool, pot or pan, just make it. It takes a little time, a little thought, and produces the most satisfying results—most of the time. And on rainy days, it's fun to do. Here are twelve good ideas to get you started:

1. *Green stick broiler* (Fig. 1). Find a large forked green stick and bend the longer end around other fork and tie to handle. Then weave green twigs, fairly straight ones, in and out until it resembles a tennis racket. You may reinforce with wire at the top of racket.

FIG. 1
Green Stick Broiler

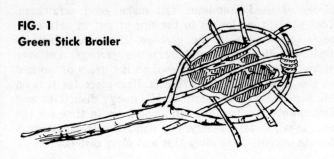

FIG. 2
Foil Pan

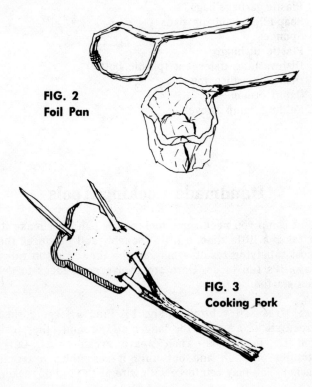

FIG. 3
Cooking Fork

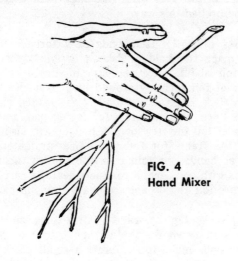

FIG. 4
Hand Mixer

FIG. 5
Double Boiler

For a hinged, turnable broiler, make two of them and hinge together at top with wire. Hot dogs, hamburgers, steaks may be broiled this way.

2. *Foil Pans* (Fig. 2). Lash ends of a forked stick together to make the holder. Take a double layer of heavy-duty foil about twice the size of the opening. Fasten edges of foil securely around loop formed from lashed green stick. Use the butt end of the forked stick for a handle. Form shallow circle for frying pan, and a deeper circle of foil for stew pan. A hanger will also do for forming the frame for foil pans. Use straightened hanger end as handle, or fold over for shorter, firmer handle. Cover with pad—metal conducts heat. Be careful not to puncture foil and do not use heavy items in pans.

3. *Cooking Fork* (Fig. 3). Take a fairly thick stick of green wood, split down the middle about four or five inches. These ends make tines. Insert a small piece of wood or a stone to keep the tines apart. Lash fork by whipping rope or string around just below split to keep stick from splitting too far. Use as long-handled barbecue fork.

4. *Hand Mixer* (Fig. 4). Select a green wood forked stick about 12 to 15 inches long. A green stick with double forks near the end is even better. Put top end of stick between palms of both hands and rub briskly back and forth using all ten fingers to twirl speedily. This is great for mixing pancake mix or eggs when you need a handy beater right now.

5. *Double Boiler* (Fig. 5). If you have to melt butter or chocolate, or heat a milk sauce, a double boiler is just the ticket. Take two sizes of empty tin cans. Put several small stones in water in the larger can, set the small can inside on the small stones, and presto you have it. Use care in removing from the fire. The metal will be very hot.

Pot Hooks

FIG. 6

Dingle Stick

6. *Dingle sticks, pot hooks* (Fig. 6.) Use these to hold pots over the fire while you take a hike before supper. Dingle sticks are long sticks about four to five feet. Set one end in the ground, fastened with rocks or forked stick. The other end will be supported in the upright forked stick, the pot will hang most often at the end of the dingle stick over the fire to cook. Pot hooks are about six inches long and notches at each end to do a good job of holding pots on cranes over the fire.

7. *Pan Tree* (Fig. 7). If you set up camp to stay awhile, why not make yourselves a handy pan tree? It allows pots and pans and cloths to dry better in the sun as well. Cut off branches from a dead, but solid tree. Leave small stubs of branches for pegs to hold pans. Drive shaft firmly into ground near your cooking area.

8. *Hobo Stove* (Fig. 8). The greatest invention ever is the miniature hobo stove. It makes the best bacon and egg breakfast you ever had. What's even better, two to four campers make their own "mini" fire and "maxi" breakfast on these. Take a No. 10 tin can. All camp kitchens have them. Using tinsnips, put a small door at the open end of the can. At the sides of the can just below the top, use a triangle pop can opener to make several "V" cuts near the back of the can to let the smoke escape. That's all there is to it. Trench candles and buddy burners may also be used for heating hobo stoves (See Fig. 15).

9. *Fire Tongs* (Fig. 9). Use these when you want to move hot coals or rocks and don't want to use your kitchen utensils. Take a strong, green sapling stick about two to three feet long. Shave near the center of the stick or heat to bend and form into a "U" shape. Lash two sides of the stick together just above the base of the "U" to form the desired shape of the fire tongs. Make two or three different sized jobs.

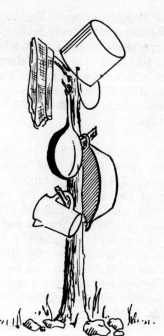

FIG. 7
Pan Tree

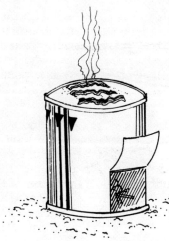

FIG. 8
Hobo Stove

10. *Popcorn Popper* (Fig. 10). Open a large juice can with regular can opener leaving lid attached to can. Take a large green pointed stick, pierce through one side of the can about two inches down straight through both sides of can. The pointed end should come through the other side of the can for an inch or two. Pour in a little oil and a little corn and you'll have yourself a can-full in no time.

11. *Cups, Ladle* (Fig. 11). Again you'll need the tin-snips, some gloves, and perhaps pliers and a small hammer. Take a No. 2 can, cut down one half inch each side of the seam until the desired height of cup is reached, turn snips and cut around can. Bend back the handle carefully to form a cup handle. Bend the edges of the cup with the pliers and hammer these down to form a lip around the cup. Make a ladle the same way, but use a smaller can and bend the tin handle around a long wooden stick for a ladle handle. Tin items must be washed carefully before use and dried well afterwards. They rust easily.

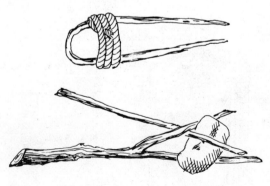

FIG. 9
Fire Tongs

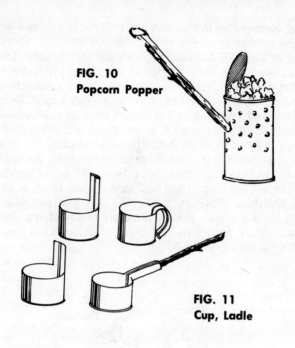

**FIG. 10
Popcorn Popper**

**FIG. 11
Cup, Ladle**

FIG. 12 Spring Box

12. *Homemade Refrigerator* (Fig. 12). If you run out of ice or that good ice chest leaks on you, it's always good to know of another way to keep things cold. This requires: (1) A cold stream or river nearby, and (2) a strong wooden box, or maybe just a good stout string. Be sure the items you want chilled are well sealed—cans of fruit and fruit juices are best. Butter or milk should be well sealed in plastic over the paper coverings. Submerge the box in water near the shore. Attach the sign, "Do Not Remove" to discourage adventuresome campers. Often campers will keep their pop cold by tying the cans or bottles to a string and submerging them in the cold riverbed. When they want it, they just pull it in. Many bottles can be tied at intervals to one string. Just be sure glass bottles do not break and stay away from where bathers may walk.

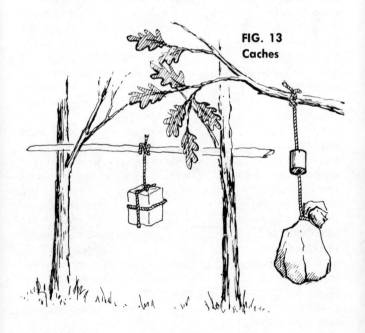

FIG. 13
Caches

The Campfire Stove

Whether you're canoeing the crest of the white water, trudging down a dusty trail, or cruising in a camper, there's always one "smarty" in the group who'll say, "When are we going to stop and eat? I'm starved!" Suddenly everyone concurs and the vote to stop is unanimous.

Quite often you may not have a portable stove handy or you don't want to take time to set it up. A small fire in a roadside grill or a small campfire may be all you need. And you can be ready in no time if you know the rules.

Contrary to what some modern camp enthusiasts say, a butane stove is not the only answer. What if the stove doesn't work? What if you run out of fuel? I have never been at any campsite yet where there was not enough kindling lying on the ground to make a good campfire. Remember cooking fires should be small. Campers who clean an area for the fire, glean small fallen twigs and branches, and bury all ashes when they leave, should make the ecologist rejoice that some are trying to keep America beautiful.

Large camping groups, such as outriggers from established resident camps, need a good campfire for teaching skills to campers in camp crafts—selecting a site, type of woods, piling such, laying the fire, preparing the stove top, preparing the food, cleaning utensils, and cleaning up the fire site.

A campfire stove costs nothing, cleans up easily, gives charcoal flavoring free, and tosses off added warmth for body and soul.

In wet weather the good camper has his wood under some tarp, or has a trench candle, or a few dry fuzz sticks for getting a good fire started.

If you are not an old hand at setting up a super cooking fire, here's how.

Selection of a Site

Remember, you will no doubt have to obtain a fire permit to build a fire of any kind, so check this before you proceed.

A good idea at this point is to get organized. Designate some campers to collect fire materials, while one or two prepare the fire site.

Consider two things first: Save the woods. Save the sod.

Four surfaces can best be used for building fires: rock, sand, soil, or sod. The first two are probably best. Soil is most often used by campers, and sod occasionally. When using sod, remove wedges of sod and replace afterwards in areas which are grassy or planted.

Never build on humus in which fire can travel underground to pop up quite a distance away. Never build in dry grass or on the roots of a tree or against a tree, log, stump, or near a bush or under overhanging branches.

Look for an open area, clear a space, ten to fifteen feet in diameter. Now you are ready to construct your fire and camp stove.

There are many different ways to build a campfire, all of them good, but each designed for a specific purpose (See Figures 16—21). Campers usually use the one-circle lay, but good woodsmen may use the two-circle lay which is also called the "keyhole."

Collect large stones, preferably with flat tops. Lay these in a circle large enough for the fire or in a double connecting circle, one large and one small. Build about six to eight inches high. On sand, dig a hole for the fire, then rocks or bricks need not be more than four inches above the ground. If on sod, remove carefully and lay it in the shade, dig down three inches. When finished, turn under the bed of ashes with a shovel, return the sod, press down gently, and water it. In each case make the lay so that your cooking grate will rest on rocks about four inches above the bed of coals.

If you build the keyhole type, the large circle can be

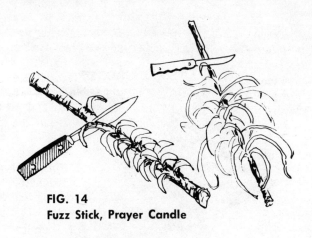

FIG. 14
Fuzz Stick, Prayer Candle

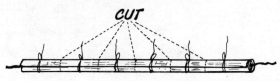

CUT

PARAFFIN

Buddy Burner

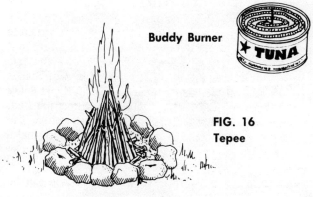

FIG. 16
Tepee

33

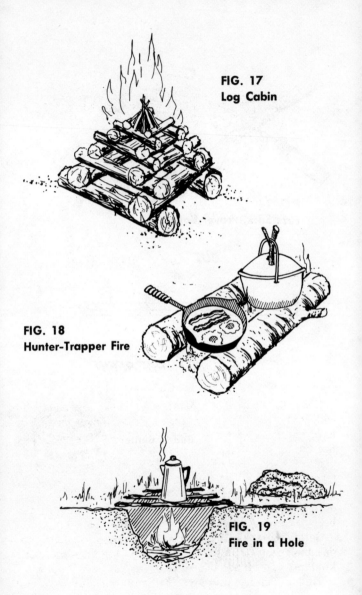

**FIG. 17
Log Cabin**

**FIG. 18
Hunter-Trapper Fire**

**FIG. 19
Fire in a Hole**

34

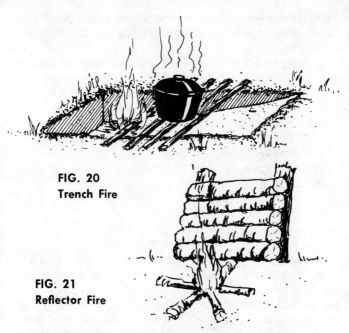

FIG. 20
Trench Fire

FIG. 21
Reflector Fire

used for sitting around, and you can rake coals from this fire into the small circle for cooking.

Selecting Firewood

Hopefully you have sent the young troopers out to collect the right kinds of fire material and by now they have carefully piled it in separate stacks around the fire lay.

Make sure they know before they start that living trees are *out*. Steer them to standing dead trees, dry dead limbs hanging or lying on the ground. Tree stubs or stumps, heavy limbs or logs are also good. On the beach, use driftwood.

Gather three types of wood and burning materials, designated according to size: tinder, the smallest; then kindling; then firewood.

Tinder can be anything that will burn quickly and

35

start the fire—dry leaves, weeds, pine needles, pinecones, small twigs or birch bark. Nothing thicker than a pencil thickness will do.

Kindling can be small, dry branches, small chunks of wood, or wood shavings, up to a thumb's thickness, and no longer than a foot. Fuzz sticks are great. They are easy to make. Get a dry stick about 12 to 15 inches long. Notch shavings into it from one end to the other, being careful not to cut off the shavings. They will look sort of like porcupine quills (See Fig. 14).

Finally comes the fuel, or firewood, the bigger stuff that makes for a great fire and great coals. Choose sticks or boards split from larger logs, two or three inches thick and about 18 inches long.

Building a Fire

The basic fire form around which all types of fires are built is called a "tepee" or "wigwam" because of its shape. First, gather a fistful of tinder and place it in the middle of three small sticks forming a tripod in the center of a circle of stones. At this point you may want to use two Y-shaped sticks that lean into each other forming a beginning tepee. Add kindling piece by piece, leaning against the upright sticks. Gradually increase the size of the wood from little finger size to arm size (two to three inches thick).

If you have built it properly, the fire should start and flare up immediately. If you have increased the size of wood too rapidly, the tinder will burn and die leaving the large logs unburned. Then tear it down and start again. Be sure to use plenty of tinder and kindling or the large logs will not catch fire. Newspaper may be used, but remember that crumpled "fire balls" of newspaper are at best a fast tinder. Building a fire is relatively easy, once you get the hang of it.

Lighting the Fire

Take dry, kitchen-type matches and go to the side of

the fire lay away from the wind, also called the leeward side. Light the tinder. If the wind is strong, protect the flame with your hands. If there is no wind, blow gently on the beginning flame.

It is best to keep matches in a covered tin can to protect them against moisture. Or you may coat them with wax, especially if you're making trench candles (See Fig. 15). A trench candle is what you use to get a fire started in wet weather. To make them, roll up one section of newspaper tightly, lengthwise. Tie with string about every four inches, leaving an end of string to burn as a fuse. Then cut through the newspaper between the strings. Dip the sections, holding the fuse end, into hot melted wax in a pan. When they are coated, set them out to dry. Take these along in a plastic bag for hard to light fires. A buddy burner is similar in use, and can double as a small fire under a hobo stove (See Figures 8, 15).

Finishing the Stove

When the fire is well burned and there are many hot coals, it's time to place the grate on the stones for the stove top. Spread the coals evenly for a large meal with more than one pot or pan. If the coals begin to cool, push them together to concentrate the heat. If the chief cook is not quite ready when the coals are, keep the fire hot by adding a piece of wood at a time. Never build a fire larger than you need.

When using a permanent fireplace, private or public, remember to have the fire four to five inches from the grate. Unfortunately, grates that you find in most parks are 10 to 15 inches high. Place rocks, bricks, or stones to build it up before making the fire.

Cleaning the Stove

No scouring pads, no scrubbing, just a bucket of water and a stick are needed. Before leaving your cooking fire and moving on, pour plenty of water on the coals, then stir them with a stick to be sure they are well extin-guished. If you are staying nearby and using an evening fire for morning breakfast, you don't need to do this. But be sure the dying coals are well protected from blowing away or spreading.

Hints for Outdoor Cooking

Most camp counselors aren't accustomed to cooking for a group of hungry youngsters and so here are some shortcuts to fill those empty tummies faster, and to get on the trail again.

1. Campers tend to resist cooking food thoroughly, especially if it's stick cookery and everyone's really hungry. Cook meat evenly by turning it often. Haste may mean raw meat and sick campers.

2. An interlocking knife, fork, and spoon are best for each camper on long trips, especially when backpacking.

3. Use and reuse foil. It can be used as pot top covers, as a cookie sheet, a cooking pan, frying pan, and a colander when holes are punched in it. It's invaluable for aluminum foil dinners and desserts. Used foil can be crumpled and used as a scratcher. When taking extra foil, roll it on a stick.

4. Take along nested plastic cereal bowls, cups, and tumblers. Tupperware items are the most practical. They have tops and can double as storage containers.

5. Convenience foods, such as modern packaged, dehydrated, and freeze-dried foods are good for long trips. They are less bulky and lighter, a must for backpackers and canoe trippers.

6. Nutrition is a must at all times with young campers. Plan good, nutritious meals including the four basic food groups each day.

7. Vegetables are a problem. Fresh, frozen, and canned

ones are not feasible for various reasons. Your best bet are freeze-dried vegetables. Some may be obtained at local grocery stores. Others can be secured from camping outfitters. Complete menus for breakfast, lunch, and dinner are available in packages with servings for four to eight. You can get chicken or beef stew, Spanish rice, chili con carne, steaks, chops, potatoes, vegetables, scrambled eggs with ham and hash brown potatoes. Family campers may go for ham a la king, shrimp creole, lobster Newburg, chicken la scala or beef stroganoff.

8. With all dehydrated and freeze-dried food, liquid is added only when it's ready to be cooked. Rain or high humidity may ruin food in cardboard boxes, so before the trip, transfer store-bought "instants" to moisture-proof, spill-proof containers which can withstand moisture and rough travel.

9. Glass jars are taboo. Use plastic containers.

10. If you use a portable ice chest, limit use to perishable foodstuffs—fresh meat and dairy products. Eliminate milk cartons by using powdered milk. A pound of margarine or butter may be kept cool and fresh outside the chest in a double-sealed plastic container or wrapped in a moist newspaper and kept in a cool place. Most cheeses do not need refrigeration and actually taste better when not icy cold. Peanut butter, jams, and syrups of all types need no refrigeration. Dry sausages, smoked hams, and slabs of bacon, can be kept without ice in a foam cooler or sealed wooden box.

11. Raw hamburger, cubed steak meat, chicken, pork chops, and pork sausage, should be used within a day when kept in a cooler. Hot dogs, processed smoked ham, and large cuts of meat can be kept longer. Keep fresh meat closest to the ice and well wrapped to stay dry. Dampness adds to spoilage. Once meat is cooked, you can store it safely for a day or two, but it's best to use it up at lunch the next day. Chill the cooler before

using and freeze meats before leaving on trip for longer effectiveness. Open the cooler as little as possible for constant and cold temperature. Cold means 40° or below. If you can't keep them either hot or cold, *don't take them.*

12. Avoid foods that spoil easily. Delete such items as custards, potato salad, coleslaw, kidney bean salad, and sandwich spreads made with mayonnaise or salad dressing. Salad mixes complete with salad dressing are now available in freeze-dried form.

13. In hot weather, eliminate sliced cold cuts. Concentrate on sausage meats or canned luncheon meats. Small tins of chicken or ham take up no cooler space and little space elsewhere.

14. You can get plastic egg cartons economically at camp outfitters. Most campers do not have these, but rather pack eggs in flour for travel.

15. If fresh vegetables are used, do not let them stand in water longer than necessary, for vitamins are lost. Add vegetables to boiling salted water and cook quickly. Do not overcook. Remove when tender. Cook longer only for soups or stews.

16. Skin tomatoes quickly by scalding them with boiling water (perhaps the unused dishwater) or holding them over flames until the skins crack.

17. When melting chocolate or measuring syrups, grease container to keep them from adhering to the sides.

18. Test eggs for freshness by dropping them into water. If they fall quickly, they are very fresh. If they sink slowly, hard-boil for safety. If they float, they are probably rotten.

19. If you need a rolling pin, use a bottle, jar, or large tin can.

20. A little vinegar and water boiled in utensils where fish have been cooked removes the fishy odor.

21. When using dried fruits for breakfast, soak and let stand the night before. Dried milk for cereal will be better if made earlier as well.

22. To test bread or cake for doneness, stick a straw or a sliver of wood into it. If it comes out clean, it is done. If sticky or doughy, it needs more baking. Remember, bread may be baked on hot stones, or on sticks. Cake is best done in a reflector oven.

23. Leftovers and refuse attract insects and wildlife. Tidy up immediately after each meal. Collect refuse in plastic bags and discard in receptacle if provided. Otherwise, we repeat, burn burnables and bury the rest.

24. Heat dishwater before you sit down to eat. A plastic dishpan or large pot will hold enough hot sudsy water to wash. Another one can hold the hot rinse water. To dispose of dishwater in the wilderness, pour it into a small pit, away from the campsite, then cover well with a layer of soil.

Lightweight Foods

Powdered eggs, milk
Dried soups (chicken, onion, potato)
Powdered cocoa in packets or cans
Freeze-dried coffee
Instant tea, hot or iced
Instant puddings, pie fillings in many flavors
Powdered juice in small paper cans (orange, grape)
Instant packets of sloppy joe mix, salad dressing,
    rice and meat seasonings
Tiny bouillon cubes for quick soups
Instant dessert mixes
Instant drink mixes—lemonade, orangeade, Kool-Aid
    flavors, apple cider and many others

If the lightweight instant food products you like come in glass jars, be sure to transfer them to plastic bags or other weather-proof containers. Big independent grocers and most chain stores carry all that has been mentioned, and new products appear every week, so look around for what's best for you.

Common Cooking Measures

3 tsp.=1 T.
16 T.=1 c.
1 c.=½ pint (pt.)
2 pts.=1 quart (qt.)
4 qts.=1 gallon (gal.)
2 T. butter=1 oz.
2 c. butter=1 lb.
4 T. flour=1 oz.
4 c. flour=1 lb.
4 c. cocoa=1 lb.

#½ can=1 c.
#1 can=1½ c.
#2 can=2½ c.
#2½ can=3½ c.
#3 can=4 c.
#5 can=5 c.
#10 can=1 gal. (12 c.)

2 c. granulated sugar=1 lb.
3-3½ c. brown sugar=1 lb.
3-3½ c. powdered sugar=1 lb.
3½-4 c. cornmeal=1 lb.
2 c. rice=1 lb.
2-2½ c. dry navy beans=1 lb.

Guess measurements:
2 finger pinch—⅛ teaspoon
3 finger pinch—⅓ teaspoon
4 finger pinch—1 teaspoon
    fistful—¼ c. for girl, ½ cup for man

Outdoor Cooking Measurements

Fire temperature. Slow fire: 250°-325°, hold hand over fire 10 seconds. Medium fire 325°-400°, hold hand over fire 5 seconds. Hot fire: 400°-500°, hold hand over fire 1 second. Hold hand where food is to be cooked to test heat.

Jiffy Pack Lunches

The excitement of packing and setting out on a camp-out leaves no time for cooking, and a lunch is just the thing to take. Or if after striking the tents and breaking camp, you're too tired to cook, stuff those leftover goodies in bags for the long ride home. You'll usually have more food than you need. Always save a candy bar or some cookies and fruit; they are quick picker-uppers and hit the spot. Or if you're taking a canoe trip or long hike, a tasty lunch is always welcome.

Sometimes it's hard to decide what to take and what will be tasty, so here are some pack lunch ideas. As a general rule, be sure to prepare a balanced meal. Include a meat or substitute, bread or bun, vegetable, fruit or sweet, and drink.

Sandwiches

It's best to butter the bread to prevent soggy sandwiches and sorry campers. Use meat that won't spoil if overheated. Peanut butter, jelly, bologna, and thin-sliced chipped beef make good fillings. Most precooked thin-sliced meats are delicious. They come in beef, ham, turkey, and chicken. More moist meats can be taken along in a plastic bag and sandwiches can be made on the trail.

43

Moist fillings are more tasty, but be sure each sandwich is tightly sealed in a plastic bag. Spread fillings to the edges of the bread and the crusts will more likely be eaten, too.

Substitutes for sandwiches are: a chunk of cheese, a hard-boiled egg, salad in a roll, crackers or Rye Crisps with fillings, or a paper cup of salad.

For variety in sandwiches, use one slice of white, one of brown, one of rye, or one of pumpernickel. Make double-deckers and give each a half.

Fruit
Fresh fruit is best, especially the kind that will quench thirst—oranges, apples, peaches (not too ripe), pears, tangerines, or grapes. Grapefruit is too large, and has little food value. Use other fruit unless you're in Florida country or on a diet.

Dried fruits such as raisins, prunes, apricots, or figs are also good and nutritious. One handful is plenty.

Vegetables
Carrots, celery sticks, and radishes, cleaned, cut, and wrapped in plastic bags usually keep if the weather isn't too hot. Lettuce and pickle in the sandwich or taken along separately to insert later make for a "dinner in one" sandwich. Fresh lettuce, washed, and broken into pieces, stored in a plastic container, makes a great salad with the addition of a small plastic packet of salad dressing.

Sweets, But Not Too Sweet
Firm sponge cake, pound cake, firm cookies, maple sugar candy, chocolate bar (except in warm weather), nuts, or wrapped hard candy are suitable. Prepackaged cupcakes, fruit pies or cookies are good for short trips, but a little expensive.

Drink
Put milk, water, fruit juice in a vacuum bottle or canteen. Frozen drinks are just right if you remove them

from the freezer just before leaving. Campers should be warned against drinking lake water or at fountains along the way.

If hot drinks are desired, add a packet of hot chocolate mix, or a teaspoon of either instant coffee or tea to a cup of boiling water.

Packets of lemonade, orangeade, or apple cider may be prepared for groups at the site by just adding cold water according to the directions on the package. Some mix right in the packet. Pop, when warm, tastes flat and is a poor choice unless the bottles can be put in a cold stream about an hour before drinking them.

Instant Menu Ideas

Breakfast

The latest and greatest thing to hit the market is granola for breakfast. It comes packaged by several companies and is advertised as 100% natural cereal. It combines oats with honey, coconut, nuts, dates, wheat germ, raisins, etc. It's so crunchy and tasty you can eat it for snacks. What's even better, you can make it yourself if you have the time.

GRANOLA

    3 c. rolled oats
    3 T. corn oil
    4 T. wheat germ
    ½ c. pretoasted coconut
    ½ c. minced walnuts, or
       pecans
    1 c. seedless raisins

Mix oats and oil, spread out in shallow pan, bake 250° until golden, about 30 min. Mix in other ingredients, cool. Store in covered container. Mix in sesame seeds or honey if desired.

For a good hot cereal, select oatmeal in one-package servings with such flavors as apple, cinnamon, brown sugar, or honey. When traveling, put packets in heavy plastic bags to seal from moisture. All you add is boiling water, about ½ to 2/3 cup. I find that covering it briefly after adding water causes it to become more firm. In addition to milk and sugar you may want to add some freeze-dried banana flakes for the perfect oatmeal topper.

Eggnog is different, but a tasty quick breakfast. Beat up one egg in a glass, add milk, pinch of nutmeg, few drops of vanilla extract or chocolate if you desire. Drink along with eating a piece of buttered toast which you have just roasted over the campfire.

French toast is a camper favorite. Take 3 eggs, beat well. Add 2 c. milk, salt and pepper. Immerse day-old bread, muffins, or rolls in the egg mixture, fry in hot skillet. Turn until both sides are golden brown. Serve with butter, syrup, or powdered sugar. Makes 20-25 slices.

Salads

Tested and tried recipes for salads are always a welcome treat to the hungry camper. Here's one:

CAMP TRIP EASY SALAD
(Serves 8)

1 pkg. freeze-dried vegetables
1 medium head fresh lettuce
½ c. oil and vinegar dressing
   Salt and pepper

Prepare vegetables, set aside. Thoroughly wash lettuce in cold water which enlarges it and makes it crisp, then break apart carefully. Drain vegetables, combine with lettuce. Add enough dressing to moisten. Toss lightly, season and serve.

Stuffed celery is another camp favorite. Fill with peanut butter, cheese spread, or cream cheese. For more zest, add ground nuts or chopped olives to the spread before stuffing the celery and yourself.

For a walking salad, each camper selects a firm eating apple, cores the center and fills the hole with cheese, raisins, nuts, peanut butter, cottage cheese, or some combination of these. He may eat it at the table or on the trail.

Carrot salad variations: Select firm carrots, one for 2 to 3 people. Scrape off the skin, cut with straight or crinkle cutter into four-inch strips. Eat as finger food, smear with peanut butter, or cut up into ½ inch pieces and combine with raisins. For more elegance, add crushed pineapple (drained), or shredded coconut.

The key to easy salads in camp is to use what you have and make the best of it. Even leftover cooked vegetables can be made to look colorful and good with dressing on top. If you take along perishable salad items such as tomatoes, lettuce, or cucumbers, use those first and save the carrots, celery, cauliflower, and radishes for later.

Wash the greens thoroughly in cold water, drain, then pack in a plastic bag or plastic container (such as Tupperware) or a lettuce crisper. Don't put your greens right on top of the ice; it will freeze them and they will wilt. If greens do get a little warm and look limp, don't throw them out. Immerse them in cold water and they'll become fresh and crisp again.

There are many kinds of dressings, but they are usually either tart or sweet. Tart ones, such as Thousand Island, onion, or Italian, are used primarily on vegetables. Sweet dressings such as Russian or French or sweetened mayonnaise should be used on fruits.

Some tart dressings you can make are: bacon drippings with lemon juice; chili sauce; mayonnaise, chopped pickle with lemon juice; mayonnaise and mustard; mayonnaise and horseradish.

Some sweet dressings you can make are: sour cream and honey; sour cream and preserves; whipped cream cheese and jam; catsup with brown sugar; whipped cream cheese and dry orange drink powder.

Suggestions for salads requiring tart dressings are:
lettuce, carrots, celery, radishes
lettuce, tomato, cucumbers
lettuce, onion flakes, pepper pieces
lettuce, bacon bits, cauliflower

pork and beans, green pepper, onion
peas and carrots, radishes, celery (diced)
green beans, kidney beans, onion
tomato, onion, green pepper
cucumbers, onion
corn, dill pickle, bacon bits

Suggestions for salads requiring sweet dressings are:

apples, dates, nuts
apples, pineapple, marshmallows
apples, cheese, celery
fruit cocktail, celery
strawberries, pears, grapes (green)
blueberries, peaches, pears
carrots, raisins, peanuts
raspberries, peaches, nuts
orange sections, pineapple, celery

Desserts

Stick cookery provides some instant goodies: Somemores, Robinson Crusoes, Marguerites, Fudgemallows (see section on Stick Cookery for recipes).

Instant mixes for puddings are delicious if you add some garnishment. To chocolate, add chopped nuts; to vanilla, add berries; to lemon, add coconut or chopped graham crackers. Coconut cream and butterscotch taste better with chopped nuts or chocolate bits.

For a special treat at camp, make a pie.

PIE CRUST
Crush 1½ c. of wafers (chocolate, vanilla)
   or graham crackers
Add ½ c. melted butter or margarine
Add ½ c. sugar

Press into pie tin, set in cooler for 15 min.

FILLINGS
Use can of prepared pie filling or prepared instant pie filling. Instant pudding fillings can also be used. Garnish top of pie with nuts, berries, coconut, extra graham cracker crumbs or wafers.

Here's a delicious dessert that feeds twelve:

HEAVENLY HASH
1 can or freeze dried package of each—peaches,
  pears, pineapples
3 oranges
1 small pkg. of small marshmallows
1 can condensed milk

Drain fruit, chop, dice oranges, mix in milk and marshmallows,
stir and serve.

To go with the hash, how about some frosted cookies?
Buy a can of readymade frosting at the grocers. It comes
in chocolate, white, cherry, lemon, and other flavors. Or
make your own with a box of confectioner's sugar and
1—2 tsp. of milk to spreading consistency. Spread between two vanilla or chocolate wafers to make sandwich
cookies.

Take leftover donuts or stale cake and create a new
dessert. Prick top and bottom with fork, pour juice
(orange, pineapple, or grape) over donut. Let stand a few
minutes, turn, let stand. Top with nuts, coconut, pudding,
or ice cream topping.

Or put hard baked goods in bowl, top with instant
pudding combined with whipped topping, leave overnight in cooler.

For an easy rice pudding, cook 1 pkg. pudding mix,
adding ½ c. of each: quick-cooking rice, more milk, and
raisins. Cook until bubbly, pour into serving dishes and
cool.

Marshmallow variations: Dip in water, roll in crushed
corn flakes, crispy rice cereal, or flaked coconut, toast
over coals. Or, dip in water, coat in sweetened chocolate
mix, then in nuts, toast until bubbly and soft.

For a crispy chocolate treat: Melt 1 pkg. semisweet
chocolate bits, add 1 c. crispy rice cereal, ½ c. raisins,
mix well. Drop by spoon on waxed paper. Cool.

For a peanut-butter jelly stick treat, spread 1—2 inch
piece of banana with peanut butter and jelly or jam. Put

on thin stick. Top with another banana piece, roll in brown sugar. Cook over hot coals until sugar melts. Eat with fork.

Parfait ideas: In individual glasses or dishes, alternate instant puddings with jellies, jam, preserves, or ice cream sauces. Add crisp cereal, cookie crumbs, or chopped nuts for topping. Example: Butterscotch pudding, chocolate topping, rice cereal; or chocolate pudding, strawberry jam, and cookie crumbs.

A final peach idea: Peel and cut up 3 or 4 fresh peaches, mix with ¼ c. honey. Prepare vanilla pudding mix as directed, fold in peach mixture, serve in individual bowls. Eat immediately.

Straight From the Grill

Grilling foods is no doubt the quickest and easiest way to cook over a campfire. But it really isn't as simple as it looks. The secret is to have the charcoal flavor without charcoaled meat.

When meat cooks, fat drips into the fire and flames leap up to char and blacken the meat. This is good if it doesn't happen too often. Otherwise you will have burned, *uncooked* meat. So before grilling, trim all excess fat from the meat, especially pork. Use lean ground beef if possible.

The first step in grilling is to wait until the coals are ash-grey and very hot and pushed together in an area just larger than the food you are cooking.

Hot coals are good for steak and ground beef, while medium coals are best for chicken and pork. If you put your hand over the coals and you can't keep it there three seconds, you know it's hot. Your hand could stay over medium coals, about 300°, for possibly four seconds. You can leave your hand over low heat, long enough to count to ten.

Slash the fat on the sides of a steak so it won't curl.

Don't puncture the steak with a fork when turning. A pair of tongs is best to keep all the good juices in. Make a pair of tongs if you don't have one (See Fig. 9).

Chicken pieces do best when you grill them bone-side down first. The bone distributes heat throughout the whole piece.

There are many items you can grill. Try your hand at some different things such as ham slices, ducklings, and all kinds of seafood.

Two other ways to grill: Use a hinged grill with long handles which you can buy at any hardware store. Or, something like it is a tennis racket broiler (See Fig. 1). You can make it yourself. It holds smaller items that might slip through the grid you have over the fire. The second way is to put your food on long skewers or sticks and broil some kabobs (discussed a little later in this book).

Of course, the average camper will not have a big juicy steak to grill most of the time. "None of the time," did I hear you say? Well, here are some suggestions on fixing what you have.

MINUTE STEAKS
(for 8)

The camp cook can often let you have a stack of these for a short trip and a fairly small group.

8 minute steaks, ¼ inch thick
Rolls or bread and butter
Seasonings and fixings

Grill 2 inches from hot coals for four or five minutes on each side. Butter rolls or bread and toast on grid next to meat. Slip meat when done into bread, salt and pepper. May add slice of cheese if desired.

If you're having a Hawaiian luau, the cook may let you have a little pork. Maybe some chops (which you could try stuffing) or a large ham. Perhaps it's too much to hope for a real roast pig complete with apple in his mouth.

51

Ham and Pork Variations

For a canned ham: Mix 2/3 cup of honey and 2 t. cinnamon, set aside as baste. Place ham on grill 4 inches from medium coals. Cook 45 minutes until thoroughly heated. Turn and baste often with cinnamon-honey glaze.

For pork chops: Trim fat from sides. Place on grill four inches from medium coals, allow about 10 minutes on each side. Brush with glaze.

For stuffed pork chops: Mix 1 c. croutons, ½ c. finely chopped nuts, 2 T. instant minced onion, 2 tsp. dried parsley, dash of chili powder, add to mixture of ⅓ c. margarine, 1 tsp. water, ¾ tsp. salt. Slit thick chops on side, stuff with mixture, use toothpicks or wood slivers to seal. Place on grill four inches from medium coals. Cook about an hour, turning several times. Baste with apple jelly during the last half hour.

For lamb or veal chops: Fix same as pork chops. Grilling time will vary according to thickness of chops. If chops are less than 1 inch thick, they will take ten minutes on each side. But if they are two inches thick they will take 20 minutes each side.

Once we had a big luau and we had to fix chicken for the whole camp, so we got an old set of bed springs, dug a big pit in which we built a fire, then put the springs over top (on ground level) and placed dozens of chicken pieces on the springs. With several bottles of barbecue sauce we kept them pretty well basted. And when we could grab a minute, we wrapped some scrubbed potatoes in foil and slid them under the springs to bake in the coals. What a great time we had!

For Mexican chicken: Split chicken in halves or fourths. Combine sauce of tomato sauce, 1 tsp. parsley flakes, 1 tsp. sugar, 1 tsp. salt, and a pinch of chili powder, pepper, and Tabasco. Put bone-side down and cook 25 minutes, baste with sauce, turn and cook 30 minutes longer. May turn and baste more often.

For Hawaiian chicken: Quarter chickens. To barbecue

sauce add ½ c. honey, 3 T. lemon juice, 2 T. soy sauce, dash of garlic salt and ginger. Cook bone-side down, grill five inches from medium coals for 30 minutes each side. Baste often.

For Italian chicken: Cut chickens in pieces, brush with oil. Put on grill, baste with combination of tomato sauce, oregano, and butter, or margarine. Chop olives fine in sauce if desired.

If you happen to be a lucky fisherman while camping, bring your catch back to camp for a hearty meal.

For grilled fish filets: Clean and filet your fish. Wash, pat dry; brush with salad oil. Put on greased grill or in hinged grill several inches from medium coals. Grill six minutes on each side, or until fish flakes easily with a fork. Baste often with mixture of melted butter and 2 T. of lemon juice. Frozen fish filets are equally good this way but take longer to cook.

If you're really game, you can just clean your fish, and stuff it with a handy vegetable filling such as this:

VEGETABLE STUFFING

1 c. chopped onion
¼ c. butter or margarine
2 c. dry bread crumbs
1 c. minced carrots or celery
1 c. minced mushroom pieces
½ c. parsley flakes (optional)
2 T. lemon juice
1 egg
2 tsp. salt
Dash of pepper

Cook onion in butter until tender, stir often. Mix remaining ingredients, add to butter mixture. Stuff fish or other selected meats. Leftover stuffing may be rolled in foil and baked over coals about 20 minutes.

Don't be afraid to grill vegetables right along with your meat for a complete meal. All you might want to add is a tossed salad.

For potatoes: Scrub and slice about ½ inch thick slices, you needn't peel them. Cut on the diagonal for a nicer slice. Parboiling them first is optional. Baste with butter. Takes about 25 minutes each side if you start with raw potatoes.

For frozen potato products: Wrap in foil with butter, salt and pepper. Grill four inches from hot coals for 20 minutes. Turn once.

For corn: Use fresh corn. Remove large outer husks; turn back inner husks, remove silk. Brush well with melted butter, replace inner husks, tie with wire. Roast on grill three inches from hot coals for 25 minutes. Turn often.

For onions: Select large, firm onions. Place washed onions on grill four inches from medium coals. Cook for 40 minutes or until tender. To serve, squeeze soft whole onion out of blackened crust.

For sweet potatoes: Cook right in coals as with white potatoes, then cut off charred crust to eat. Or you may cook in skins until slightly tender. Then remove from water, slice, baste with butter or Italian dressing, grill over hot coals, 8—10 minutes each side.

For acorn squash: Put directly in coals as with potato, roast one hour. Turn often. When done, cut in half and remove seeds, fill with sweet sauce (marshmallow, brown sugar, butter). Or you may cut and seed the squash first, place face down first to heat thoroughly, then put bottoms down for last half hour. Cook on grill three inches from hot coals. Fill with butter and brown sugar when done.

For tomatoes: Cut tomatoes in half crosswise. Sprinkle top with salt, bread crumbs, and shredded cheese; dot with butter. Place on grill four inches from medium coals, make foil tent over them. Cook about ten minutes.

Skillet Cookery

The aroma and sound of sizzling bacon in a hot skillet is irresistible to the waking camper. And who doesn't like to watch juicy hamburgers frying or fresh-caught fish turning to a golden brown in a skillet? Just about anything you can cook at home can be done at camp.

Be sure that the skillet is very sturdy and has a heavy handle. Cast-iron skillets are best, with heavy aluminum coming in second. A heavy skillet lined with Teflon is an extra blessing, if you can afford it for camp use.

Shortenings which come in areosol cans such as "Pam" are handy on the trail. Check your grocer's shelves.

Sun-Up Fixin's

Fried Eggs: Sprinkle a little flour on pan bottom after shortening for crisp, brown-bottom eggs.

Scrambled Eggs: For light taste, add ¼ c. milk or cream to 6—8 eggs, beat well, add salt, pepper, 1 T. of sugar, bacon bits (Add nutmeg, if desired).

Omelet: Beat 4—6 eggs in large skillet, or 2—3 eggs in small skillet, add 1—3 T. milk, seasonings. Cook slowly until done on top and bottom, lifting sides to let eggs cook thoroughly. When almost done, fill one half with cheese slice, jelly, bacon, or ham; flip one half over other half. Cook slowly for 2—3 minutes.

Pancakes: Prepare in bowl or shaker from boxed mixes. Add blueberries, strawberries, chocolate bits, raisins, or nuts for variety. Vary between silver dollar size for little ones to plate size for men.

Sandwiches: Toast peanut butter sandwiches. Spread slices of bread with peanut butter, spread with any flavor jelly or jam; sprinkle with raisins or slices of banana. Spread outer face of bread slice with butter. Toast in skillet until golden brown. Variety: Dip sandwiches in beaten egg and fry, instead of spreading with butter.

Fish: For a special treat, season fresh whole fish or filets with salt and pepper, fry in bacon grease until brown, about 5 to 7 minutes. Serve with scrambled eggs, toast and coffee.

Sandwich Fillings

Hot dogs: Roll frequently to prevent burning, best to cook on a stick. (See Stick Cookery and Fun With Franks.)

Hamburgers: Though expensive, ground chuck is a better buy than hamburger because it has less waste. (See Stick Cookery and Hamburger Heaven for recipes.)

Ham slices: Fried bologna is good as a substitute for ham. Call it a "pork roll" sandwich. Add baked beans on bun. For leftover ham, add Swiss cheese.

Bacon: Combine with tomato and lettuce, or cheese and lettuce. Fry it with chicken livers and serve on a bun for a change.

Cheese: Grill between buttered bread slices with hot dog pieces, lunch meat, or bacon slices (cooked).

Egg: Boil hard and make egg salad by adding slight amount of salad dressing. Fried-egg sandwiches are delicious. Use beaten-egg coating for sandwiches before frying.

Chicken: Cook, cube, add to chopped celery, salt, pepper, mayonnaise, spread. Beat two eggs, and 2 T. water, dip both sides of sandwich into mixture, then into crushed cornflakes. Fry in hot greased skillet until brown.

Tuna: Drain from can, add chopped sweet pickles, spread on bread, add one slice of tomato, toast in skillet.

Use choice of canned spreads, add own favorites, toast in skillet.

Meat and Vegetables

Sausages: Prepared links keep longer than fresh bulk pork. Sliver links and serve with scrambled eggs or vegetables. Chop and add to pancake dough. Fry with baked beans.

Liver: Tear or cut off salvage edges, roll in seasoned flour, shake off excess, fry slowly in lightly greased skillet, 5 minutes each side. Longer cooking makes it tough. Bacon grease or bits in skillet give added flavor. Add onion rings. Use medium coals.

Chops: Ham, lamb, pork, with or without breading. One-inch thick sliced chops are great grilled right over the fire. Serve with jelly, apple slices, pineapple chunks or rings.

Potato: Slice paper thin for American fries, dice finely for hash brown, cut sticks for French fries, fry in ¼ inch oil in skillet, turn often. When brown, drain, add seasonings, bacon or ham bits, serve.

Fruits: Fry slices of apple, tomato, or pineapple.

Vegetables: Pieces of cauliflower, miniature whole potatoes (from can), fried rice mix, corn and potato fritters, onions, squash.

CATCH A CHICKEN
(Serves 6)

⅔ lbs. frying chicken, cut up
6 T. salad oil or butter
2 pkgs. spaghetti sauce mix with tomatoes
3 c. water
2 T. dried, minced onion
1 oz. dried mushrooms

Brown chicken pieces slowly in hot fat, turning them until they are brown on both sides. At the same time, mix remaining ingredients and mix well. When chicken is browned, pour sauce over it. Cover and simmer until chicken is tender. About 30 minutes. More time should be allowed if coals are not hot.

CRUNCHY CORN DOGS
(Serves 3)

1 c. pancake mix
2 tsp. sugar
½ c. water
½ lb. hot dogs
finely crushed corn chips

Combine pancake mix with sugar and water; mix well. Dry hot dogs. Dip hot dogs in batter, then roll in corn chips, coat thoroughly. Fry in small amount of hot fat until golden brown.

INDIAN CORN

½ lb. sliced bacon, cut up in 1-inch pieces
1 can whole kernel corn
8 eggs
Dash of pepper

Fry the bacon until crisp, drain off fat. Add drained corn. When this begins to boil, break in the eggs, one at a time. Add pepper. Stir gently until eggs are scrambled and firm. For an added touch, put cheese on top, cover for a minute or two, and serve.

MULLIGAN STEW

1-2 onions, cut up in small chunks
2 c. water
1 can corned beef, cut up
1 can peas
Salt, pepper

Boil onions in water for 5 minutes. Add remaining ingredients, boil slowly over coals until onions are done. Don't overcook onions or they will become mush.

SPANISH BURGERS

2 lb. ground beef
1 onion, chopped or 3 T. minced dry onion
1 can chicken gumbo soup
3 T. catsup
3 T. prepared mustard or ½ tsp. dry mustard
½ tsp. salt
¼ tsp. pepper

Brown beef with onion in skillet. Add remaining ingredients and simmer for 15 minutes. Add a little water if mixture is dry. Serve on toasted buns or biscuits.

SKILLET PUDDING

1 can evaporated milk
¾ c. of prepared chocolate
½ c. sugar (unless sugar included in chocolate)
¾ c. water
Graham cracker, cookies, etc.

Put first four ingredients in a skillet and bring to a boil, stirring constantly. Add broken-up cookies or graham crackers, cover and cook over low coals for 30 minutes, stir occasionally. Spoon into dishes. Good way to use up leftover cookies.

SKILLET BREAD

1 c. flour
1 tsp. baking powder
1 c. water
  Dash of salt

Sift dry ingredients together at home or at camp. Start warming greased skillet. Put dry ingredients in bag or bowl, add water, mix. Flour hands before handling dough. Form into round flat cake. Dust with flour and set it in warm skillet. When bottom is slightly browned, turn over and bake some more. Or you may use a reflector fire.

SKILLET DINNER

3 T. cooking oil or bacon fat
1 med. onion, sliced
1 lb. ground chuck
1 can red kidney beans
1 can whole kernel corn
1 tsp. garlic salt
¼ tsp. pepper

Fry onion in hot fat until tender, remove from skillet. Break ground beef into small pieces, brown in hot fat. When light brown, pour off fat, add onions, kidney beans, corn and seasonings. Simmer in skillet about 10 minutes.

Fun With Franks

Probably the most popular treat for campers is the hot dog. How many ways can you fix a hot dog? Here are some suggestions:

First, fry one strip of bacon (partially), set aside. Split hot dog lengthwise, but not all the way through. Now, you're ready to fill them:

> with slice of cheese
> with mandarin orange slices
> with small mushrooms
> with dill pickle
> with pineapple strip

with cantaloupe strip
with small green onion

Now, wrap up with bacon, place on grill for 10 to 15 minutes, turn often. Next, you may want to split them almost through, lay flat on grill and baste them:
with brown sugar and mustard
with pineapple syrup
with chili sauce
with garlic butter

Or, you might want to grill them straight and put the sauce on top and serve them:
with toasted garlic buns
with coney sauce in a bun
with sauerkraut on a plate
with melted cheese and butter in bun
with oregano and mozzarella cheese in bun
with favorite jam in bun

Perhaps you have another special way. Try your wildest idea, it may become a hot dog gourmet's delight.

Hot dogs or frankfurters or small sausages can be fixed in the aforementioned ways. Some you will grill, others you can pan fry, still others may be placed in foil and put on the coals.

Hamburger Heaven

Next to the hot dog, the hamburger is the most used outdoor meat at camp. Your meat can go a long way if you know how to stretch it. Nearly everyone knows that adding a few bread crumbs and milk makes a meatloaf, but what good ways can you fix hamburger that the camper will like? Try these:

BIG SMOKEY
(Serves 10)

You've heard of Big Mac, Big Chef, and Big Boy. Now meet Big Smokey, the best double-decker hamburger in the whole woods.

    2 lbs. ground beef, lean
    2 eggs
    ½ c. bread crumbs
    Salt, pepper

Mix beef, eggs, bread crumbs and seasonings, shape into thin patties (about 20). Fry on grill. When almost done, put cheese slice on one. Serve on double-decker bun, with catsup, mustard, pickle or onion.

Variations: You can put in filling and seal edges before cooking. Or you can fill

    with pickle slices, or onion slices
    with crumbled blue cheese or shredded
        American cheese
    with fresh or canned mushrooms
    with chopped celery
    with chopped nuts
    with barbecue sauce

These can also be cooked in heavy foil squares on top of coals for 10—15 minutes.

MEATBALLS A LA GRAVY
(Serves 5)

    1 lb. lean ground beef
    ¾ c. mashed potato flakes
    ½ c. milk
    1 egg
    1 tsp. salt, dash pepper
    1 pkg. brown gravy mix
    ½ c. water
    ½ c. catsup
    1 tsp. Worcester sauce

Combine first five ingredients, shape into balls about 1 inch in diameter. Roll in dry gravy mix, fry in pan. Remove meatballs from pan. Add rest of ingredients; mix well. Return meatballs to fry pan and gravy. Simmer 10 min.

LEMON BURGERS
(Serves 5)

1 beef bouillon cube	1 t. lemon juice
½ c. boiling water	½ t. salt
1 lb. lean ground beef	½ t. pepper
⅓ c. dry bread crumbs	½ t. sage and ginger
1 t. grated lemon peel	

Dissolve cube in boiling water; mix well with beef, crumbs, lemon peel and juice, and seasonings. Shape into 4 or 5 patties; chill if possible. Grill 4 inches from hot coals, about seven minutes on each side. Serve in toasted buns.

ONION CHEESEBURGERS
(Serves 6)

2 lbs. lean ground beef
1 tsp. salt, dash of pepper
1 pkg. dry onion soup mix
½ c. water
6 slices processed American cheese

Mix meat and seasonings; shape into 12 patties. Stir soup mix with water until well dissolved. Use large piece of heavy-duty foil (12″ x 12″). Put in first patty, spread with 2 tsp. onion sauce, cheese slice, second patty, another 2 tsp. onion sauce. Wrap securely in foil. Cook on coals 8—10 minutes on each side. Serve in warmed buns.

HAMBURGER STEAKS
(Serves 6)

2 lbs. ground beef or ground round
1 egg
1 med. onion, chopped or 3 T. minced dry onion
½ c. cracker crumbs
¼ c. catsup
2 t. brown sugar
1 tsp. prepared mustard
   Barbecue sauce

Mix first four ingredients. Blend catsup, sugar, and mustard into meat mixture. Divide in half, shape each to resemble a steak. Brush top and side of each with barbecue sauce. Place steaks on grill, sauce side down over medium coals. Brush steaks again with sauce. After several minutes, turn carefully. Takes about 10 minutes.

Other hamburger specials are found throughout the

book. Check Spanish Burgers and Skillet Dinner under Skillet Cookery.

Stick Cookery

Most campers' introduction to outdoor cooking includes some type of stick cookery. It puts everyone to work right away and is a good learning experience.

First of all, everyone must find a green stick about two to three feet long. Take a trusty penknife, cutting away from you, making a pointed end about five inches long. For hot dogs, Somemores, Kabobs, Angels on Horseback, make a point, little-finger size or smaller. For Doughboys and Pioneer Drumsticks make sticks thumb size.

Green wood can be identified if it bends easily without breaking. Find sticks on the ground before stripping young saplings. Two or three campers may share a stick if green wood is scarce. Do not use dry, brittle wood or you'll lose the food when the stick burns through and the flames lick it up.

A good substitute for a green stick is an old coat hanger, straightened, bent in half, ends twisted together. But remember that metal conducts heat so protect your hands with a pad, thick hankie, scarf, or glove.

Cook over a good bed of hot coals, not flames. Flames scorch and give meat only the appearance of being cooked, especially in the case of Pioneer Drumsticks. Tell campers to cook them longer than they think is necessary for a most delicious hamburger treat.

Clever campers lay the stick across a rock over the coals and the other end down with a rock or forked stick.

For impaling hot dogs or sausages on sticks, put them on diagonally for easier handling (See Fig. 22).

When toasting bread for breakfast or cooking bacon as in kabobs, lace onto the stick for easier turning.

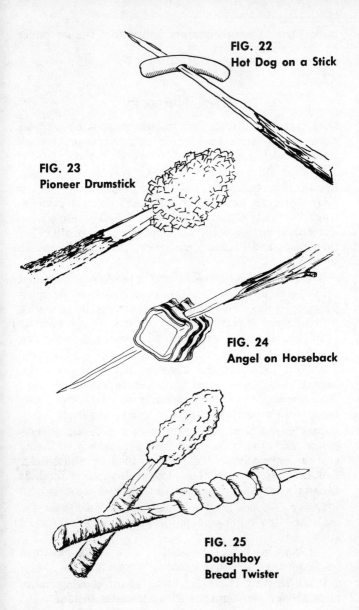

FIG. 22
Hot Dog on a Stick

FIG. 23
Pioneer Drumstick

FIG. 24
Angel on Horseback

FIG. 25
Doughboy
Bread Twister

PIONEER DRUMSTICKS
(Serves 8)

2 lbs. ground chuck (or hamburger)
2 eggs
   Salt, pepper, onion flakes
1 small box of cornflake crumbs (or crushed cereal)
2 pkgs. hot dog buns (8 pack)

Mix beef, eggs, and seasonings thoroughly. (May add cornflake crumbs to mixture or use to roll in.) Wrap a small handful around end of stick, squeezing evenly. Make it long and thin, not into a ball. Roll in cornflake crumbs. Cook slowly over coals, turning often. Twist slightly to remove from stick, put in hot dog bun. Add mustard, catsup, and relish (See Fig. 23).

ANGEL ON HORSEBACK
(Per Person)

1 inch squares of firm cheese
1 slice of bacon
1 lettuce leaf
1 hamburger bun each
   Salad dressing (optional)

Thread one slice of bacon on sharpened stick, partially cook. Then wrap bacon securely around chunk of cheese. Cook until bacon is done. Serve with lettuce and dressing on bun (See Fig. 24).

BREAD TWISTER
(Cave women cream puff)

Prepare Bisquick dough according to package directions. If a bowl isn't handy, mix dough in paper bag. Roll out flat, ¼ to ½ inch thick, but in 2 inch wide strips, about six to eight inches long. You may use a pop bottle or pop can for rolling pin.

Bare the stick to the pulp (twice the size of your thumb, you may also use a clean broom handle). Warm and flour the stick, wind strip of dough spirally around stick, leaving slight gap.

Bake for 10—15 minutes over coals, turning often. Slide off stick, fill with butter, jelly, peanut butter (See Fig. 25).

DILLY DOGS

Take one hot dog, slit partially lengthwise, insert slice of cheese, wrap one slice of bacon around, fasten with toothpicks or wood sliver. Place on stick, cook over hot coals. Serve in bun.

65

DOUGHBOY
(1 batch)
Make exactly like Bread Twister, but instead of cutting dough in strips, take a small handful and form over end of stick and down the sides like a handle covers the top of a baton. Cook same as Bread Twister, slide off and fill with favorite filling. Might like to try cheese for a change (See Fig. 25).

PIG IN A BLANKET
Take one hot dog, impale it on thin green stick, cover hot dog with biscuit dough (see above recipe). Bake over coals about 10 minutes. Dip in catsup or mustard when done. Looks and tastes much like a corn dog. For more corn dog taste, use corn meal muffin mix. Remove about half of the liquid so it will stick to hot dog.

BACON TWISTER
Cook bacon or sausage thoroughly on a stick. Cover with thin layer of biscuit dough. Bake 10 minutes over fire coals. Serve with eggs in morning or use as a snack.

Stick Cookery Desserts

SOMEMORES
Carefully brown a large marshmallow on a stick over the coals. Prepare one square of a graham cracker (½ cracker) on which you place 4 small squares of a plain chocolate candy bar. Remove marshmallow from stick, place on chocolate and graham cracker. Cover with one more square of a graham cracker (other half). Squeeze together and take a big bite. You're in for a sweet treat. Then you can judge for yourself whether you want "Somemore."

FUDGEMALLOWS
Prepare a marshmallow as above. Instead of chocolate bar, use a can of fudge ice cream topping, the kind that comes with an extra plastic cover. Spread fudge topping on graham cracker, place marshmallow, then another graham cracker. If using whole graham crackers, roast two or three marshmallows, lots of fudge topping for a super sweet treat.

ROBINSON CRUSOE
Same as above, use peanut butter instead of chocolate.

NUTTY DOGS
Same as above, but roll in chocolate and nuts. Can use a strong chocolate sauce instead of chocolate bar melted.

MOCK ANGEL FOOD

Cut up day-old bread into 2-inch squares. You may want to remove the crust. Place bread on stick. Dip in dish of sweetened condensed milk, then in dish of coconut, coat evenly. Bake over coals until nice and tasty. Sweet but good.

EGGHEADS

Take day-old donut, cut into bite-sized pieces, dip in beaten egg mixture, toast over coals. Or dip donut pieces in cocoa, toast and eat.

CHEESE BALLS

Make small recipe of Bisquick biscuits, roll flat, cut into 1 x 3-inch strips. Wrap around 1—1½-inch cheese square, covering completely. Put on stick, cook over coals 5 minutes or more.

SHAGGY DOGS

Take one plain chocolate bar, melt in foil cup. Prepare 1 cup coconut. Toast large marshmallow, dip in chocolate, then in coconut for a special treat.

ANGELS' HALOS

Take one large glazed donut, place marshmallow in center. Run stick through side of donut and marshmallow. Toast both over coals, serve with hot chocolate on a cool evening.

DOUGHBALLS

Mix 1 c. Bisquick with ½ c. margarine, ¼ c. water. Form into small balls, place on stick, bake over coals. When evenly browned, dip in melted margarine or butter, then in a sugar-cinnamon mixture.

MARGUERITES

Roast one marshmallow very brown. When done, put with nut meats between soda crackers. A new twist to the sweet Somemores.

DATE DREAMS

Take pitted dates or date halves, alternate with large halved marshmallows (snip with scissors) on a green stick. Toast slowly over the coals. Serve on crackers, in bananas (dug out like canoes), or in cored apples.

Up to this point, we have been talking about cooking on a single green stick. But it is possible to cook many of these items on a forked stick or a wire fork (made from coat hanger). Not only is this good if you have a special friend for whom you want to cook a special sweet treat, but it works well to use a two-pronged stick for heavier items such as steaks.

Hot dogs, sausages, bacon, toast, apples, chops, or even sandwiches can be done this way. For best results, run the tines of the fork into the food lengthwise or lace to hold the food securely while roasting and turning.

Kabobs

Perhaps this is one of the oldest ways to cook food. Before there were forks or even tables, men speared meat, cooked it over the campfire and ate it when it cooked slightly. This is about what we do when we make shish kebab or broil meat on skewers. The more common term is "kabobs."

Expensive skewers are not necessary at camp. You can make your own. Make one from coat hanger wire or from a green stick. A double-wire skewer is better (bend hanger in half, make handle, scrape off paint). If you use a single wire, bend it in half so that the food won't turn on the wire as you cook it. The loaded skewers can be rested between bricks laid on the grill over the fire. Or if you use a hunter-trapper fire, skewers can rest on the firedogs (logs on each side of fire).

Alternate meat with vegetables on skewer. Cook hard vegetables slightly in salted water so they will broil readily over the open fire. Don't crowd the skewer, so all food will cook thoroughly. Baste while cooking. Use a medium bed of coals, cook slowly, avoid flaming fire.

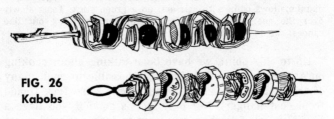

FIG. 26
Kabobs

LAMB KABOB

2 lbs. spring lamb, cubed
2 med. onions, wedge size pieces
12 mushrooms, cut to fit
1 small box of cherry tomatoes
2 green peppers, cut in wedge size pieces

Marinate meat overnight. String meat and vegetables alternately on skewers. Baste with marinade, broil until done.

CHICKEN LIVER KABOB

1 lb. chicken livers, cut in half
6 slices bacon, thick, cut in squares
12 mushroom tops
Bread crumbs
Cooking oil

Dry livers, cut up. Place one piece on skewer, then bacon square, then mushroom, repeat. Baste with oil, roll in crumbs, broil until bacon is done.

FRUIT KABOBS

1—1½ inch chunk of fresh or canned fruit such as pineapples, prunes, dates, peaches, pears, apricots,
cherries.
1 c. honey
1 tsp. lemon juice

Thread fruit on stick, brush honey and lemon juice mixture over fruit, heat over coals. Brush occasionally with butter to keep from burning. Serve with angel food squares or mock angel food.

MEAT KABOBS

1 inch square of sirloin steak (¼ lb. per person)
Small chunks of onion, or canned baby onions
Cherry tomatoes, mushroom pieces
Green pepper, cut in squares
Bacon slice to weave in and out (optional)

Put on end of bacon, then meat, then vegetables, then meat, etc. Baste if desired and broil until done. Slide off onto plate, possibly on mound of rice.

SEAFOOD KABOB

Almost any kind of fish can be used including shrimp, scallops, and lobster.

> Sea food, cut to chunk size
> 2 green peppers, cut in wedges
> 12 mushrooms, cut to size
> 5 tomatoes, cut in wedges
> 2 med. onions, cut in small wedges
> 24 bacon squares, thick cut
> Butter, lemon juice
> Seasonings

Alternate fish, bacon, vegetables on skewers; season with salt and pepper, broil until done. About 10 minutes. Push on plate, pour over melted butter and if you desire, lemon juice.

FRANKFURTER KABOBS

> Frankfurters, sliced in thirds
> Dill pickles, large, sliced
> Onions, small, sliced
> Prepared mustard

Alternate food on skewers; brush on desired amount of mustard, broil until well browned. Push contents into opened hot dog bun. Add catsup if desired.

HAM STEAK KABOBS

> Ham, cubed
> Pineapple chunks
> ½ c. pineapple juice
> Canned sweet potato chunks
> ½ c. brown sugar or honey

Mix pineapple juice and the sugar or honey until blended, warm sauce. Alternate ham, potatoes, and pineapple on skewers. Baste with the sauce, and broil until brown.

VEGETABLE KABOBS

Almost any kind of firm vegetable can be used. Since the meat often takes longer to cook, you may want to broil the meat separately and kabob the vegetables. Raw vegetables such as onions, squash, potatoes, and carrots need to be parboiled first. When half cooked, remove from water, thread on kabob, dip in oil, season, and broil over coals. Add thin slices of tomato, green pepper, or just before broiling.

Tin Can Cookery

Don't throw that tin can away, it may come in handy. Need a cup or ladle? Make one from an ordinary tin can. All of these and many more can be made from tin cans.

Tinsnips, a pair of gloves, small hammer, pliers, and perhaps a few nails will do nicely to make almost anything. Cans come in sizes from 1 to 10. No. 1 is what most evaporated milk comes in; No. 2 are the vegetable cans; with No. 3 being the large fruit containers. No. 5 is the large fresh coffee size; while No. 10's are gallon size, most often used by dorms, camps, etc.

For safety, wear gloves to prevent cuts and blisters. When making holes, as in a popcorn popper, place can over tree stump or wood block. Use a wooden post or end of a log for pounding down handles for cups, ladles, etc. Tin items rust easily, so wash and dry very carefully, use plastic scratcher to clean.

Suggested cooking utensils

No. 2 cans. Cut ½ inch each side of seam down to desired height of cup, bend back handle, pound down edges (See Fig. 11). Ladle: make like cup, but bend handle over long stick, secure cup to stick with small nails, or wire in place. Biscuit cutter: Cut off both ends, cut in half, flatten, attach handle for flipping. Candle holders: Cut off an inch or two of unopened end, or cut down sides to within an inch of end, cut out, use as reflected candle holder.

Nos. 3—5. Cereal bowls: cut off top half, pound down edges. Cooking pan: attach wire handle to lift off fire. Popcorn popper: (See Fig. 10).

No. 10. Large cooking kettle: attach wire handle. Mailbox: cut out both ends. Tray: cut off both ends, cut down seam, make flat, bend up edges, file. Hobo stove: (See Fig. 8).

Many other items for use at camp may be made with just a little imagination. If you goof, just throw it away and start again. Use an extra laundry bag to carry the tin utensils in. Be sure to use only cans that have had food in them, no paint or oil cans should be used for cooking.

Here are some recipes that you can make using tin cans:

Baked Potatoes
(Use No. 10 can)

Scrub potatoes, wrap in waxed paper, then in moist newspaper. Put them in sand in can to keep them from touching each other or the sides of the can.

Place can in hot coals and cook for 45 minutes.

Add additional coals as needed to keep hot. Keep dirt or sand in can moist, add little water as needed. If the coals die, it may take longer.

Camper's Stew
(Use No. 3—5 can, lid partially opened)

Put in hamburger patty or beef cubes, thinly sliced potatoes, chopped carrots, celery, onions, or corn. Moisten with ½ cup of water, tomato juice, or catsup. Put on lid. You may punch lid several times to let steam escape. Set can deep in hot coals, cook for 15 to 20 minutes. Provide one can per camper.

Hobo Stove Breakfast
(Use No. 10 can)

Make into hobo stove (See Fig. 8). Place over prepared mini fire (6″ diameter). Stoke fire through open door. If fire quits, remove can with hot pads, build new fire and continue cooking.

Now you're ready to place one bacon strip on top of can, fry well. If you fry several strips, remove excess grease before continuing. Be careful not to spill grease into fire. Put bacon on plate.

Eat out the center of a piece of bread, place it on top

of hot lightly greased can, turn once. Break fresh egg into center of bread. May turn over if you like them "once over."

Regular eggs may be fried on can after bacon is removed. Or you may want to scramble an egg or two. For a real treat, dip your bread in a mixture of one egg and ¼ cup milk and fry for delicious French toast. Top with butter and syrup or honey.

Aluminum Foil Cookery

Years ago when I was a Girl Scout we never heard of anything called aluminum foil. But now it's just about the best thing a camper can take along. You can cook your food in it, use it as a plate, make a cup, a pan, a bowl, a skillet, an oven, even use it for a dishpan if you sink it in the ground. I wouldn't be without a large roll of heavy aluminum foil. The heavy-duty kind is best for most camping purposes since the lightweight tends to puncture easily.

All aluminum foil has both a shiny side and a dull side. When wrapping packages of food to put in the coals, be sure to put the dull side on the outside. It absorbs more heat that way. The shiny side tends to repel the infrared rays of heat. Some foil has been developed with a black side, which, when it's on the outside, really cooks food

FIG. 27 Foil Wraps

in a hurry. But it's too expensive for the average camper. However, if you want the microwave touch with a nice browning effect on your food, it might be just the thing for you.

It's so important in cooking foods in foil to seal them properly before placing them in the coals. You want to tightly seal in the steam and juices, at the same time keeping out dirt and ashes.

There are a couple of ways to fold foil cooking packs. The first is started like you fold a sandwich in wax paper. Bring up the two ends to the middle top and fold down twice, then roll each end and bring final fold up on top so all three folds are on top. Now it's ready for the coals, with all folds up. Another way is to bring two ends to the side, fold two or three times until tight to side, then roll ends up, same as before. Perhaps one advantage to the second method is that you could turn it frequently thus cooking evenly on both sides.

For the perfect "tv dinner," wrap your foil package of food a second time with heavy foil. That way, when the outer foil is removed which is covered with dirt and ashes from the fire, you have a clean inner foil package to open out and use as a plate.

When many campers are making their own dinner and there are many foil packages in the fire, each camper gets a kick out of crimping the foil a certain way to make that "special shape." This way he can recognize his own dinner as it's cooking. Most often he has put in a little extra potatoes, or a pat of butter, for his own special dinner treat.

Turning foil dinners is done with a stick. With the stick you can adjust it over the best coals and push it in when the outer coals grow cold. It's used to pull it out of the coals when done. If you've brought along a lot of equipment, you may want to use a pair of tongs instead, or you may have made a pair of fire tongs as mentioned earlier. Once the foil package is out of the coals, its outer covering cools quickly and you can pick it up shortly. If you're not sure it's done, open it carefully before pricking the vegetables with a fork because you don't want the ashes to fall in your dinner.

How the coals are prepared to cook these and how long it takes varies. Some stack coals, cover with ashes, then put the packages on. Others put packages in coals, and cover with coals so they won't have to turn them. If the coals are very hot, cooking time will be cut considerably. If you cook beside the coals, it will take longer. A timetable of cooking with foil is included at the end of this chapter.

One caution to new campers is to watch the foil packages carefully. If the coals are very hot and if you're new at this business, the food may burn. If the outside is getting very black, it's time to take it out immediately. The usual foil dinner takes about 15 minutes. Some new campers like to rush their meal and take it out when the vegetables are still raw. One way to avoid this is to cut the potatoes, carrots, onions, etc., into very small pieces, then they will cook faster and be done the same time as the meat. If you're cooking vegetables alone and do not have an item with natural fat in it, better stick in some butter, margarine, or ½ slice of bacon for that good flavor, and succulent taste.

Foil Cooking Utensils

Here are some tips on how to make foil items for use around the campfire. In Fig. 2 you'll see a foil pan you can make. But that's only a beginning. Foil utensils may not be the best you could use, but when it's a case of having a disposable item that you don't have to clean, and when you have plenty of foil on hand, it can't be beat.

There are a couple of ways to make a good cup for a hot cup of chocolate or a cool drink of lemonade. The easiest way is to double the foil (about 12"—15" square) and then double your fist, put it in nearer one side, crimp the foil around it.

Fold down the edges to make a tight smooth rim and

twist the rest of the foil into a handle. Another way is to make a double-layer square and press it around the end of a can, crimp down the edges tightly to make the rim and twist the handle into place. If you want a large cup, use a larger can.

For handles for these cups, use a wire coat hanger. Bend or cut off hook, then bend in half. Form middle of wire around can of same size as desired cup, twist securely, bring two ends back, use pliers and twist at end to form long handle. After holder is made, slip cup in (made over same size can) and fasten edges to rim of hanger.

If you want to make a plate, place double-layer foil square around the top of a sawed-off log or tree stump, crimp up edges to form round plate.

To form a rectangular pan for baking biscuits, or to place as a drip pan under chickens on a spit, lay a double sheet of foil flat, and bend up the edges with a straight edge or sharp fingernail. Have sides about one-inch high, fold over corners, crimp to make secure.

With a coat hanger and some more foil you can make skillets of two or three sizes. The smallest one can be made the same as you make a cup with handle. The only difference is that the foil cup is more shallow, depressed about an inch to an inch and a half. This is the perfect sized skillet for melting butter for popcorn, sauteing chopped onions, or poaching an egg. For the latter, fill foil with water, when boiling, crack an egg into it. When egg is cooked, pour off water, slide the round-formed egg onto a buttered piece of toast, salt and pepper.

To make a large skillet, just bend a wire hanger into a square. Twist handle down for easier handling. Take a double length of heavy foil, fold over, slip wire between, crimp edges. When cooking, it will depress slightly holding in juices. Lighter items such as bacon, eggs, pancakes, fish, and thin-sliced meats do nicely in this skillet. Best of all, it can serve as a plate and is disposable.

Now let's look at some good recipes to use in these foil containers. The first one is a camp favorite, probably the one everyone learns first.

SALISBURY STEAK DINNER

Use a regular foil 12″ square, and a heavy foil square 12″—16″ for each person.

Form hamburger patty
1 handful thinly sliced potatoes
1 handful thinly sliced carrots
1 slice onion (if desired)
1 pat butter (or margarine)
Salt, pepper
Add sliced mushrooms or celery (if desired)

Lay out thick foil square, place one patty in center. Pile vegetables on top, and 1 pat butter. Fold up all sides. Wrap again in heavy foil square. Crimp into "special shape." Place in coals (not flames), turn once after seven minutes. Remove after about 15 minutes in all. Open, check to see if vegetables are done, season to taste, eat with fork.

DOUBLE CHEESEBURGER

Use 1—2 large heavy-duty foil squares per person.

2 patties of ground beef
Onion slice or chopped onions
Slice of Cheddar or American cheese
Salt, pepper

Place cheese and onions on one patty, cover with second patty, salt and pepper to taste. Wrap up in foil, cook on coals, turning at least once. (See Pizzaburgers in Reflector Oven Cooking.)

STUFFED FISH SPECIAL

Large double square of heavy foil.

4—5 fresh fish
Bread crumbs
½ cup nut meats
1 apple, chopped fine
½ cup celery
Salt, pepper

Clean fish thoroughly, prepare stuffing. Chop all ingredients and combine, stuff fish, season. Seal up, wrap in foil, cook in coals.

HAM DINNER
Use two 12½"—16" foil squares for each person.

        Generous ham slice for each
    2 small slices of canned sweet potatoes
3—4 pineapple chunks each
   ½ inch slice of apple
        Butter or margarine
        Raisins (optional)
        Salt and pepper
        Brown sugar

Place apple slice in first, fill with butter or raisins, put in ham slice, sweet potatoes, top with pineapple chunks and brown sugar (if desired). Wrap and wrap again. Place in coals about five minutes on each side. For a full course dinner, add corn (off cob or from can).

MEATBALL STEW
Use two 12½"—16" foil squares for each person.

   3 small meatballs (ground chuck)
   3 or 4 small canned potatoes (drained)
   1 or 2 canned onions (drained)
Salt, pepper
   3 T. condensed soup (tomato sauce if no soup)

Place meatballs and vegetables together in foil square. Sprinkle seasonings and sauce over all. Fold at center and at ends. Wrap again. Place on hot coals for 20 to 30 minutes.

Substitute other meats in the first three recipes to suit your taste. A pork chop would do well in the ham dinner, or you might try lamb chops, fish, or fondue meat.

CHUCK ROAST
Large double square of heavy foil.

   3—4 lb. chuck pot roast
    1 cup of sliced potatoes
   ⅔ cup of sliced carrots
   3—5 onion slices

Sear meat first on both sides over grate, put in foil, add vegetables. Package carefully. Wrap it well to retain all juices. This will probably take one hour. (See Chinamen's Chops in One-Pot Meals.)

BROILING A STEAK

Place steak on foil, place on coals. Do not wrap. Turn steak once. Length of time depends on how well-done you like your steak.

FISH DINNER

Use two large foil squares per person.

1 fish filet (fresh or bought)
1 slice lemon
1 slice bacon
1—2 slices of onion, potato
   Worcester sauce
   Salt, pepper

Place bacon slice in first, then fish, then lemon, top with onions and potatoes and a dash of Worcester sauce. Season to taste. Wrap package securely. Wrap again, put in coals. Turn frequently while cooking.

Potato Treats

Hash browns: Grate 3 potatoes onto foil; add bit of onion flakes, 2 chunks of butter, 2 T. of cream or milk. Seal in foil, cook for 30 minutes.

Stuffed potato: Clean potato and core like an apple, stick in a link sausage. Wrap in foil and cook for about an hour.

Vegetables in Foil

Baked potatoes: Wash and wrap individually in 2 layers of foil. Bury in medium coals, bake for one hour. Use splinter of wood to see if done or squeeze to see if soft.

Corn on cob: Pull back husks, take out all silk, spread with butter. Replace inner husks, discard outer husks. Place each ear in square of heavy foil, roll up, twist ends. Roast corn on medium coals about 15 minutes, turning once.

Peas: Place frozen bag of peas in foil, top with butter and almonds, wrap well. Cook on medium coals about 20 minutes.

Carrots: Cut off ends, scrape clean. Slice or chop carrots into small pieces, pile in center of foil, add butter.

May add sugar if sweet taste is desired. Wrap and place in medium coals for 30 minutes.

Onions: Cut off ends, peel. Set in foil, season, add pat of margarine or butter. Wrap in double foil, twist ends. Takes 30 minutes. Another way is to slice them and pile them in foil, take a shorter time to cook. May add Worcester sauce before cooking.

Peppers: Remove seeds, stems, membranes, place on heavy foil, fill with Spanish rice mix. Wrap securely. Cook over medium coals 15—20 minutes.

Sweet potatoes: Wash, scrub or peel (medium size best). Cut in half, scoop out some. Fill with butter, brown sugar, dash of cinnamon, nutmeg and allspice. Close up, wrap up, cook in coals for one hour. Turn frequently.

Summer squash: Wash, take off top stem, cut in half. Scoop out seeds, fill with brown sugar and nut meats, or with bacon and onions (chopped). Season with butter. Put halves back together, cover completely and tightly in foil, put on medium coals for 40—50 minutes.

Cabbage: Select small head, cut out stem, fill with seasoning and butter. Place on a large sheet of double foil, gather around loosely, twist at top. Cook slowly on or beside coals for one hour. If chopped up, takes only 30 minutes.

Fruits in Foil

Baked apples: Select Golden Delicious or good cooking apple (not tart). Core and fill with a selection of two or more of the following: small marshmallows, English walnuts, cinnamon candies, brown sugar, pineapple chunks, or raisins. Dot top with butter. Don't core it all the way through if you want the good stuffing to stay in. Place apple in a large square of heavy foil, bring ends to top, twist and place in medium coals. Takes about 30 minutes.

Banana boats: Select one firm banana for each camper. Strip back one peel of banana skin, scoop out banana like a canoe. Fill space with small marshmallows and chocolate bits. Put back peel, wrap in foil. Leave in coals about 3 minutes on each side, or less time if you want just the stuffing melted. Open and eat with a spoon.

Fruit salad: For each serving, put slice of pineapple on square of heavy foil. Heap fresh strawberries or blueberries on top. Sprinkle with a little sugar (confectioner's preferably). Wrap up, put in coals for about 5—10 minutes. Open and serve with whipped topping or nuts.

Hot grapefruit: Cut in half, seed and section. Pour 1 tsp. honey on top with a pinch of nutmeg or cinnamon. Wrap up securely, cook for 3—5 minutes.

Spiced peach delight: Take two well-drained canned peach halves. Fill one with cinnamon candies, chopped nuts, sprinkle with lemon juice. Place other half on top. Wrap whole peach securely in heavy-duty foil square. Place on medium coals for five minutes on each side. Take from coals, open and serve with whipped topping.

Fresh peach delight: Select medium sized ripe peaches. Wash and cut in half, remove pit. Fill cavity of one with fresh blueberries or other berries, sprinkle with brown sugar and 1 tsp. lemon juice. Wrap up in foil. Cook about six minutes on each side.

Bread in Foil

French bread: Take 1 lb. loaf, sliced into one-inch slices, fill with a butter or cheese spread (listed below).

Vienna bread: Cut into one half-inch slices, fill with spreads.

Large individual club rolls: Split in half, fill with butter spread.

Spreads: Melt ½ to 1 stick of butter or margarine, combine with

—garlic powder or crushed clove

—dried minced onions

—2 tsp. of dried parsley leaves, pinch of oregano, 2 tsp. of grated Parmesan cheese and salt

—1 to 2 tsp. of seeds such as celery, dill or sesame

—shredded cheese, pinch of parsley flakes, 2 tsp. of Worcester sauce.

When bread is filled, wrap securely in heavy foil. Place on medium coals, heat 10 minutes, turning often.

To summarize on the newest and best ways to cook at camp, here are cooking times for foil cookery:

Meats

Beef, hamburger	10-12 min.
Beef, cubes 1″	20-30 min.
Chicken, cut up	20-30 min.
Hot dogs	5-10 min.
Pork chops	30-40 min.
Pigs in blanket	15-20 min.
Fish, whole, cleaned	15-20 min.
Fish, filet	10-15 min.

Vegetables

Carrots (sliced)	15-20 min.
Potatoes (whole)	45-60 min.
Potatoes (sweet)	45-50 min.
Potatoes (sliced)	10-20 min.
Corn (ears, whole)	5-10 min.
Acorn squash	25-30 min.

Miscellaneous

Apple (whole)	20-30 min.
Banana (whole)	5-10 min.
Biscuits (space to rise)	20-25 min.

Reflector Fire Cookery

Since you can make your own reflector oven out of aluminum foil, here are some suggestions on how to use it. This kind of baking is used outdoors for breads, pies, cakes, biscuits, pizzas, and a host of other things. It requires only a means of reflecting heat onto the top of the food to brown and cook it while heating from beneath as well.

Reflector ovens can be purchased from camp outfitting companies. They fit into a compact carrying case and fold flat for storage. Or you can make one out of tin cans, by cutting in half a large rectangular can and inserting a shelf in the middle. Or you can make one out of aluminum foil.

The crudest kind is just a rectangular pan as described in the previous chapter. Fill with refrigerated biscuits, corn meal mix or filled foil muffin cups. Place on grill, then make tent of aluminum foil over pan. Allow some space to peek in to watch them bake. The heat will reflect from the shiny foil and bake them. This method can be used on any grill or rack over medium coals.

An oven that works as well as the commercial kind can be made from foil, too (See Fig. 28). First, take a four-foot piece of heavy-duty foil. Cut two green sticks a foot larger than the foil is wide, sharpen the ends. Lay the sticks at each end of the foil, roll several times until foil is securely around them. Drive ends of sticks in ground, keeping foil taut and sticks leaning at about a 45° angle. Set this about 8—12 inches from fire on leeward side, so ashes blow away from food, angle toward the ground (where fire will be). To cook, set wood on windward side of fire so the fire's heat will reflect down

FIG. 28
Reflector Oven

83

onto the food. Keep reflector clean and free from soot, the shiny side must reflect.

When using a commercial oven, make the fire as high and as wide as the oven, keep flames about even with the shelf of the oven. Place items to be baked on the shelf when it is sizzling hot for best results. Baking temperature will be about 375°. To control the amount of heat, vary the distance between the oven unit and the fire. Frequent rotating of the food on the shelf will help give more uniform baking.

Reflector Oven Specials

Potatoes: Scrub white potatoes or sweet potatoes. Grease them with margarine. Bake them in reflector oven for 45 min., test for doneness.

Meats: A small chicken basted with butter, set in a square foil pan will brown up nicely in about an hour.

Orange shell bakers: Hollow out one half of an orange, leaving only the thick peel. Mix up mashed canned sweet potatoes with brown sugar and small marshmallows, bake in orange shells. Or, break an egg in them, set them in oven to cook, season to taste.

Rolls, biscuits: Use prepared ones. They come in plain rolls, buttermilk, cinnamon, orange, pecan, and many other kinds. They must be kept cool until use, but will do nicely in a round cake pan or foil pan which you have made.

Cakes: Use a package mix. Snackin' cake is great for the reflector oven because it can be mixed and baked in an 8-inch square pan. Make a heavy-duty foil one for the occasion if you like. Pineapple upside-down cake comes out nicely too and is a real treat with a ham dinner or a luau.

Pies: Any fruit pie, especially in a tart shell, does nicely. Frozen pies are cumbersome to carry along, unless you plan them for your first meal out.

Cookies: For a special children's treat, slice up some cookie dough which you've kept in the cooler, put on foil in reflector oven and bake. Or melt a sweet topping on some stale cookies or grahams for a quick treat.

Desserts: Somemores can be made to end that meal on a sweet note. See recipe in Stick Cookery. Banana Boats also can be made in the oven. See Aluminum Foil Cookery for the recipe.

Hors d'oeuvres: Slice hot dogs on crackers, top with American cheese square, melt in reflector oven, top with olive slice. Use various other types of crackers or small squares of bread. Top with meat spread, top with Swiss cheese, melt, serve. Be original, use a variety of spreads and toppings.

Pizza burgers: Take halves of English muffins, or bun halves. Spread with spaghetti sauce, top with cooked (drained) ground beef, sprinkle with oregano and shredded mozzarella cheese. Bake in reflector oven for 15 minutes or until cheese is thoroughly melted.

Drop biscuits: Mix 2/3 c. milk or water with 2 c. prepared biscuit mix. Drop dough on greased shiny side of heavy-duty foil. Make 8 large or 16 small biscuits. Bake in reflector oven for 15 minutes. Variations: Add 1 c. blueberries and a little sugar for special flavor. Use as shortcakes for desserts or for creamed meat sauces.

Cinnamon rolls: Make as above, but roll in sugar-cinnamon mixture before baking. Takes about 8—10 minutes. Roll small to make 24 rolls.

Coffee cake: Mix ½ c. brown sugar with 4 c. prepared biscuit mix and combine with ½ c. butter. Blend until mixture resembles coarse meal. Blend in 1 c. milk or water to make a soft dough. Pour this into a greased pan, sprinkle top with ½ c. brown sugar and 1 tsp. cinnamon. Bake in reflector oven in moderate heat for 20—30 minutes.

Corn bread: Use prepared corn bread mix, pour into greased pan, bake in reflector oven for about 45 minutes. Test for doneness with wood sliver.

Meat turnovers: Mix ½ c. milk, ¼ c. melted margarine and 2 c. of Bisquick with fork. Divide dough into 8 parts. Place each piece of dough on waxed paper; press into five-inch square. Place a thick slice of cooked or canned meat on one half of square, add pickle relish or chili sauce. Fold dough over meat and press edges together. Indent edges with fork. Make small slit on top of each turnover. Put on greased dull side of heavy-duty foil. Bake in reflector oven 30 minutes or until golden brown.

Baking in a Skillet

A second way to use a reflector fire is to reflect heat into a skillet for cooking or baking. A common recipe is Bannock Bread, also called Skillet Bread.

BANNOCK

1 c. flour
1 tsp. baking powder
¼ tsp. salt

Mix these dry ingredients together. This can be done before you leave by mixing a multiple of this recipe and by carrying the mix in a strong plastic bag. Secure opening with a fold and a rubber band.

When ready to make it, have skillet greased and fairly hot, because the dough rises quickly and the cake will lose some of its lightness if you don't work fast. Rub some of the flour on your hands, and quickly mix enough water into the mix to make a stiff dough. Pat into a cake about 1-inch thick; flour it well and set it on the hot skillet, which is then placed over a medium fire. When the cake has firmed and has begun to brown on the bottom, flip the cake over to do the other side. At this point the pan can be propped at an angle in front of the fire, so the heat will reach the top of the cake. Let it bake and brown slowly for 15 minutes or so; then test it with a toothpick to be sure it is done. Break it open when hot, and serve it with butter and jelly, or with a stew. Pancakes of all varieties can also be cooked this way.

Planking Fish

Find a flat board or split log, spread fish filets on board, peg down, prop up in front of reflector fire (See Fig. 29). Complete instructions are under Fish Cookery.

FIG. 29
Skillet Propped

FIG. 30
Standard Crane

One-Pot Meals

Probably one of the best meals to make for a large group on the go is the one-pot meal. In some cases, it can be put on hours before. It contains all the meat and vegetables that you need in one pot.

Men like this better than stick or foil cookery because then they don't have to cook their own meal. Mom and the girls or the KP committee can do the job. After working in the out-of-doors, it sure tastes good!

Most of the one-pot meals are like stews and can be served on a mound of rice, hot biscuits, or cubed bread. Here are some of my favorites:

SLUMGULLION
(Serves 5)

6-10 slices of bacon
  2 T. minced onion or flakes
  1 can of tomatoes
½ lb. cheese, diced
  2 cups of ground beef, already cooked and drained
    Salt, pepper

Cut bacon in small pieces and fry with onion. Drain off some fat, add tomatoes, meat, and salt. Cook for about 20 minutes, then add cheese cubes and continue cooking until cheese melts.

FIG. 31
Victor-Auer Crane

MACARONI AND CHEESE
(Serves 8)

2 cups macaroni (small pkg.)
2 onions (diced or dried)
1 #2 can tomatoes
1 lb. cheese, diced
   Bacon grease

Drop macaroni into boiling salted water, cook until soft; drain. Meanwhile, fry onions until brown. Add tomatoes and diced cheese. Add mixture to macaroni in large kettle and blend thoroughly over fire until cheese melts slightly.

COMANCHE (KOMAC) STEW
(Serves 4)

1 #2 can tomatoes
2 onions, diced or dry
2 eggs
8 slices toast
2 slices of bacon
   Salt and pepper

Cut bacon into small, neat squares. Fry until browned well, remove from fat. Add peeled and finely minced onions, cook until soft and slightly browned. Add tomatoes and bacon to onions and fat mixture, simmer ½ hour. Add eggs one at a time, stirring vigorously after each. Season to taste. Serve on hot toast. Use a low fire to insure low cooking temperature.

IRISH STEW
(Serves 5)

5 onions, sliced
1 lb. meat, cut in 1" cubes
5 small potatoes, cubed
5 carrots, cut in ½" pieces
5 celery sticks, cut in 1" pieces
   Salt and pepper

Melt a little fat in kettle, fry onions and meat until brown. Cover with cold water, bring to boil. Cook slowly for 1—2 hrs., add potatoes and vegetables. Continue cooking until tender, about 40 min. Season to taste. Serve over biscuits, rolls, or in bowls.

This is a good recipe to fix and leave cooking while hiking, then return to put in vegetables as you prepare the rest of the meal.

RING TUM DIDDY
(Serves 5)

6 slices bacon, diced
2 onions, sliced
1/4 lb. cheese, diced
1 #2 can tomatoes
1 #2 can corn
Salt, pepper

Fry bacon and onions until brown, pour off part of fat. Add this mixture to tomatoes and corn, bring to boil. Add cheese and cook slowly until melted. Season to taste. Serve over bread, toast, or rolls.

POT OF GROUND ROUND
(Serves 4)

1 lb. ground round (cut up)
2 T. cooking oil
2 stalks celery, cut 1/4 in. pieces
1 med. onion, sliced (or onion flakes)
1 green pepper, 1/4 in. slices
1 lb. can baked beans
Salt, pepper
Garlic powder (optional)

Heat oil in pot, add vegetables, fry until soft. Remove from pot. Add meat to pot, cook low, stir often, until meat becomes brown. Add beans and cooked vegetables, stir, cover and cook until heated thoroughly. Stir often. Add seasonings to taste. Serve with tossed salad, bread and butter.

AMERICAN CHOP SUEY
(Serves 4)

2 lbs. ground beef
1/2 cup chopped onion or 2 T. instant minced
2 stalks sliced celery
2 cans condensed cream of mushroom soup
2 soup cans of water
3 tablespoons soy sauce
3/4 soup can of Minute Rice (3/4 cup)
Dash salt, pepper
Chow mein noodles

In large pot, brown ground beef; drain. Add all ingredients except chow mein noodles. Cover and cook over low heat for 10 minutes or until rice is tender. Serve over chow mein noodles.

CHILI CON CARNE
(Serves 6)

1 cup ground beef (cooked)
3 slices bacon, cut in ½ inch squares
2 medium sized onions, diced (or dry)
1 #3 can tomatoes
1 can kidney beans, undrained
2 cups cooked spaghetti
½ t. chili powder
   Salt, pepper

Fry bacon slowly until crisp and brown. Pat in finely cut onions and cook slowly until soft. Add tomatoes, cook for 5 min. Add beans and spaghetti. Let entire mixture cook slowly for 10 min. Stir often. Serve in bowls with bread and butter.

This is a hearty meal for campers. If the campers are going on a short trip, have the cook prepare meat and spaghetti the night before, keep wrapped and cool, then you can get a good meal in a jiffy.

SPANISH RICE
(Serves 4)

1 package Minute Rice
1 chopped onion (or dry, diced)
½ c. chopped celery
1 green pepper, diced (optional)
1 #2 can tomatoes
½ lb. diced bacon
   Seasoning

Cook bacon and remove from fat. Cook onions, celery (and pepper) in bacon fat. Heat the rice with the tomatoes. Combine bacon and vegetable mixture with rice. Season to taste and simmer until thoroughly cooked. About 10—15 minutes. Note: You may substitute this recipe with a packaged mix from the store.

CHINAMEN'S CHOPS
(Serves 4)

4 pork chops
4 T. Minute Rice
1 can condensed golden mushroom or cream of
   mushroom soup

Brown chops, drain. Add rice and soup. Cover and simmer for 45 minutes. Can also put chops in with 1 T. of rice and 2 T. of soup. Wrap tightly, cook 50 min.

SOUTH AMERICAN SPECIAL
(Serves 4)

1 medium onion, sliced
1 lb. ground beef
1 #2 can tomatoes
1 tsp. chili powder
1 pkg. brown gravy mix
  Corn chips

Brown onion and ground beef in pot; drain. Add remaining ingredients except corn chips. Cook over coals about 5 minutes. Serve with or on corn chips or corn bread.

CHICKEN, MEXICAN STYLE
(Serves 5)

2 lbs. frying chicken, cut up
1 can condensed tomato soup
1 soup can Minute Rice (1 cup)
  Seasonings
1 can Mexican style or whole kernel corn, drained
½ med. green pepper, chopped

Season chicken with seasonings. Coat with flour, brown in hot fat. Add remaining ingredients. Cover and cook low about ½ hour or until chicken is tender.

Backpackers: In pot, combine 4 pkgs. freeze-dried chicken, 1 envelope dehydrated tomato-vegetable soup mix, 1 c. dehydrated mixed vegetables, or corn, 4-5 cups of water. Bring to a boil. Cover and cook low about a half hour.

POLISH STEW
(Serves 7)

6 med. potatoes, peeled, chunked
6 carrots, sliced 1 inch thick
2 med. onions, cut into wedges
½ med. head cabbage, shredded
½ tsp. salt
2 lbs. Polish sausage or hot dogs, sliced
2 cans (8 oz.) tomato sauce
2 tsp. Worcester sauce
  Dash of pepper

Boil potatoes, carrots, onion, cabbage, and salt in water until vegetables are tender. Drain and reserve 1 cup vegetable water. Add remaining ingredients plus 1 cup reserved water. Simmer about 20 minutes. May use celery instead of cabbage if preferred.

CHINESE CHICKEN
(Serves 5)

1 can (11 oz.) mandarin oranges; drain and save syrup
¾ mandarin can of water (½ cup)
3 cans (5 oz. each) chicken or 2 cups cubed cooked chicken
2 stalks sliced celery
1 pkg. chicken gravy mix
½ cup Minute Rice

Take mandarin orange syrup, add all remaining ingredients except orange slices, fry in pot. Cover, simmer 15 minutes until rice is done. Add mandarin oranges; heat up again. Let stand few minutes before serving.

Backpackers: Use 2 pkgs. freeze-dried chicken, 1 c. dehydrated peaches; omit celery, use ½ t. dry celery flakes. Combine all ingredients except water in plastic bag. When ready to cook, put contents of bag in pot, add 1½ c. water. Cover and cook low 15 to 20 min., until fruit is tender. Stir once in a while.

QUICK CHILI
(Serves 4)

2 large cans chili with beans
1 lb. wieners, cut up
½ chili can of Minute Rice (about 1 cup)
½ chili can of water (about 1 cup)
¼ cup catsup or barbecue sauce
4 T. Parmesan cheese

In pot, add all together. Cover and cook about 15 minutes. Serve in bowls or with buns.

Backpackers: Use freeze-dried chili con carne mix (12½ oz.), 3 cans of cocktail franks. Combine all in pot with water needed for con carne mix. Cover and cook about 20 minutes.

EASY CHILI
(Serves 5)

2 lbs. ground beef
1 pkg. spaghetti seasoning mix
  Parmesan cheese
1 can spaghetti sauce with mushrooms
1 can kidney beans, undrained

Put ground beef in pot with ½ pkg. dry sauce mix, brown meat. Add canned spaghetti sauce and kidney beans. Sprinkle with rest of dry spaghetti mix. Cover and cook low 20 minutes or more until meat is done. Sprinkle with Parmesan cheese.

CHILI CHEESE SOUP (POLAR BEAR'S TEA)
(Serves 5)

1 can chili with beans
1 can condensed Cheddar cheese soup
1 tsp. Worcester sauce
Dash garlic salt

Combine all ingredients in sauce pan. Heat until it starts to boil. Serve over hot dogs or spaghetti or eat plain.

Backpackers: Use 12½ oz. pkg. of freeze-dried chili con carne mix. Fix as directed, cook for 15 minutes. Then add soup, sauce, and garlic salt.

CORNY KRAUT
(Serves 4)

1 can (12 oz.) corned beef, cubed or use wieners, cut up
1 can sauerkraut, drained
1 can condensed cream of mushroom or celery soup
2 tsp. dill seed or dill flavoring
1 can peas, drained

In pot, combine all except pears. Simmer for 10 minutes. Add peas; heat up again until ready to serve.

TUNA NOODLE DELUXE
(Serves 4)

2 cans of tuna, drained, flaked
1 can macaroni and cheese
½ c. cubed cheese (Cheddar, American)
1 stalk celery, chopped
2 T. chopped green pepper (optional)
1 T. chopped onion or 1 t. instant minced onion
½ tsp. salt
1 T. lemon juice

In large saucepan or pot, combine all ingredients; mix thoroughly. Heat over coals until just heated through. Serve immediately.

MEXICAN FIESTA
(Serves 4)

1 can tamales
1 can chili with beans
1 can whole kernel corn, drained

Fry tamales in greased frying pan; remove outer casings. Add the chili with beans and corn. (Do not mix.) Cover and heat slowly. Serve with green salad.

MEXICAN BEEF AND BEANS
(Serves 4)

    1 T. margarine
    1 lb. lean ground beef
    2 T. instant minced onion
    1 can kidney beans, drained
    1 can enchilada sauce
    ¼ tsp. salt
    ½ tsp. chili powder
    1 c. Cheddar cheese, dried

Melt margarine in pan, add beef, cook until brown and crumbly; drain off fat. Add remaining ingredients, except cheese. Cover, move pan to lower heat, let cook 10 minutes. Just before serving, stir in cheese. Serve in bowls, top with corn chips.

TENAYA BEANS
(Serves 8)

    1 can luncheon meat, cut in 1 inch cubes
    1 can drained pineapple tidbits
    1 can baked beans
    2 T. brown sugar
    ¼ tsp. ground cloves

Fry meat in greased skillet until brown. Add pineapple, beans, brown sugar, and cloves. Heat slowly, stir often. Serve with brown bread, warmed in foil over the coals.

TEN MINUTE STROGANOFF
(Serves 4)

    2 pkgs. sour cream sauce mix
    ⅔ c. milk
    1 pkg. dry onion soup mix
    2 pkgs. mushroom gravy mix
    2 c. cold water
    2 cans instant meatballs

Fix sour cream sauce in a bowl, use half usual amount of milk. Set aside. Put onion and gravy mixes, dry, in a large saucepan or pot. Gradually add water, heat to boiling, stir often. Take to edge of coals. Fix meatballs according to directions. Then stir sour cream into liquid in pot, blend well. Drain meatballs, add them to sauce. Heat over warm coals for a minute or two. Don't let sauce boil. Serve over biscuits, noodles, or rice.

TUNA DINNER
(Serves 3)

3 slices bacon, cut up
1 small onion or 3 t. instant
1 can new potatoes, drained
1 can tunafish, drained
Parmesan cheese, grated

Fry bacon, add onion, cook until done. Drain and dice potatoes. add to pot; add drained tuna; heat thoroughly. Serve in bowls, sprinkle with Parmesan cheese.

QUICK SEAFOOD SPECIAL
(Serves 5)

1 pkg. Minute Rice (7 oz.)
4 T. instant minced onion
1 can stewed tomatoes
1 can (7½ oz.) minced clams and juices
1 can (4½ oz.) shrimp, rinsed and drained
1 can (7 oz.) oysters and juices

Put all in a pot, stir together, bring to a boil, cover and simmer for 5 minutes. Remove from heat and let stand for 10 more minutes or until rice is done.

SLOPPY JOE SPECIAL
(Serves 8-10)

2 lbs. ground beef
2 cans pork and beans
4 T. instant minced onion or 1 med. onion, chopped
⅔ c. molasses
⅓ c. catsup
Hot dog or hamburger buns

Fry meat in pot, drain. Add rest of ingredients, all but buns. Cook about 15 minutes. Serve over buns, eat with fork.

Some Soup Specials

Take regular cans of condensed canned soups, such as:
Tomato and add: ground beef and noodles,
            or Parmesan cheese,
            or chicken, rice, peas,
            or tunafish, onion flakes,
            or ground beef, peas.

Vegetable beef and add: cooked brussels,
　　　　　　　or sprouts and green pepper,
　　　　　　　or beef cubes, diced,
　　　　　　　or cooked potatoes,
　　　　　　　or meatballs and gravy,
　　　　　　　or diced celery, noodles.

Cream of potato and add: clams, diced onion,
　　　　　　　or ham cubes, cheese,
　　　　　　　or bacon bits, peas,
　　　　　　　or beef cubes, corn.

Bean with bacon and add: hot dog pieces,
　　　　　　　or onion flakes,
　　　　　　　or bologna, cubed,
　　　　　　　or cooked ground beef.

Just a note or two about one-pot meals. Many of the recipes given in this section could also be used for skillet cookery if you have a large skillet with high sides.

Many more soup recipes could be added here. But perhaps you have a favorite of yours you'd like for camp. Use a big pot, be sure you have plenty of meat and vegetables, and you will have a happy crew when you're through.

Ever try baking biscuits in a pot instead of in the oven? Try this: Place a metal pie or cake tin upside down in the bottom of a large heavy pot. Put cover on pot and preheat for about 5 minutes over medium coals.

Prepare biscuit mix according to package instructions and drop by spoonsful onto tin or foil-covered rack in bottom of pot. There should be about 12 biscuits. Cover immediately and return to medium coals. Check biscuits for doneness a little sooner than package directions. Remove from heat and keep lid slightly ajar to keep biscuits warm.

One final word: Every day in the supermarket you'll find new skillet dinners or "meals in one." Almost any of these would work well with a large skillet or one large pot. If you go to the expense of buying these, be careful to wrap them in foil or plastic to keep out moisture. If you remove the outer cardboard box, be sure to keep the directions. Have fun making one-pot meals!

Cooking in Coals

Many of the recipes given for aluminum foil cookery can be used for cooking right in the coals. However, there are times when unwrapped food can be placed directly on the coals. At other times, if foil is not avaliable, food may be wrapped in wet leaves, wet mud or clay before baking. Then after breaking off clay, the outer covering of the food is washed or removed and it is ready to eat.

Years ago, when foil was not available, skilled woodsmen found ways to cook food in leaves and other coverings from nature that we know little about. We know that other countries still do this today.

You might want to try a few of these after the coals are just right.

Roasting Ears of Corn

Turn back the husks from young, tender roasting ears, and remove the silks. Sprinkle lightly with salt, replace husks, soak entire ear (covered) in water for about a minute. Bake directly in coals for about ten minutes.

Potatoes

Scrub white, red, or sweet potatoes well (medium size). Place on hot coals in a single layer, not touching. Cover with coals to a depth of one inch, replenishing them frequently. Cook 45 minutes to one hour. When small sharp stick will penetrate easily, they are done. You may wish to coat with thick layer of mud or clay. It will come off cleanly when potatoes are done.

Little Pig Potatoes

Slice one end off a potato, hollow out enough of the

center to stuff a half of a sausage inside. Also use cheese, bacon bits, or raw egg for stuffing. Replace end of potato, fasten with slivers of wood, thorns, or toothpicks. Bake about one hour. Test doneness by pinching or piercing with wood sliver.

Onions

Same as regular potatoes.

Squash

Scrub and cook right in coals, turn often, bake for about one hour. Take from coals, halve, remove seeds, fill with butter and brown sugar.

Roast Apples

Core apples 2/3 way through, save top ½ inch of core. Fill opening with raisins, brown sugar, nuts, or sausage. Plug with top of core, secure with picks or thorns. Place in medium coals for 45 minutes. May also prepare in mud pack as with potatoes.

Eggs

Prick small hole through the egg shell (but not the membrane) at large end and through the other end as well (puncturing the membrane this time). Stand egg on large end close to the fire (moderate heat. Too much heat will cause it to explode). Soft eggs will be ready in five minutes, hard-boiled in 10 minutes. Eggs may also be wrapped in wet leaves, or wet mud before baking.

Fish and Fowl

Pack them in mud. With *fowl,* remove the head and feet and clean away the intestines, then cover the whole bird with clay, forming a full casing around it. Place in the coals and the bird will cook completely. When the clay is cracked away, it will take the feathers and skin with it, leaving a dressed baked bird.

With *fish,* remove the head, or not, as you wish, slit the vent and remove the entrails. Then encase in mud and treat as you did the fowl. Again, when the clay cracks off, the scales and skin are removed and you can slit out the backbone and ribs, leaving only the clean filets.

Barbecuing

We go from cooking in a pot, into the fire (coals), and now into the ground, or *pit barbecue,* also called bean-hole or emu cooking. The second type of barbecuing is *on a spit,* much like the rotisserie type done at home.

Pit barbecue is a method of cooking by steam which supplies a moderate even heat. It is really a variety of fireless cookery and the excellent results justify the long cooking time required. About three hours are necessary to cook a chicken, and a half day for a ten pound roast.

BEAN HOLE BEANS

- ¾ lb. (2 cups) dry navy beans
- ½ lb. salt pork or bacon, diced
- 1½ tsp. salt
- ⅛ c. sugar
- ⅛ c. molasses
- 2 onions, chopped fine (may use minced onions)

First, set beans to soak. They may be parboiled, to soften them sufficiently, but there is a danger of overcooking, so if you can, let them soak. In the morning, dig a hole in the ground, large enough to hold your bean pot with room to spare. Lay kindling at the bottom of the hole, then more wood, crisscrossed, until you reach the level of the ground. Then, crisscross heavier wood, preferably, seasoned hardwood, which will give you a good bed of coals. Light the hole, which should be at least 18 inches over the surface of the ground. As your fire is burning, prepare the beans.

In bottom of pot, place layer of bacon or salt pork, then put in half of your presoaked beans, add another layer of bacon and top with remaining beans. Sprinkle both layers with salt and sweetenings. Add onions with beans or leave out. Top with rest of bacon, then fill with hot water, cover tightly. Dig out coals, set in pot, cover completely with coals, bank with ashes, leave for eight hours. Result: finest beans you ever ate.

ONE HOLE MEAL

3-5 lbs. meat (beef, ham, pork)
6-8 whole carrots
6-8 whole potatoes
5-6 whole onions
    (May substitute parsnips, corn, etc.)

Dig hole about 2—3 times larger than food to be cooked. Line the sides and bottom with nonpopping rocks. Build a good fire in it, keep going for 1—2 hrs. until good bed of coals is ready and rocks are very hot. Have food prepared, take out some hot rocks and coals. Place food in pit, cover with hot rocks and coals. Cover heavily with soil for steamproof oven. May also cover with tarp and soil. Then wait for food to be done. About 8 hrs. May take longer depending upon food.

A preheated Dutch oven makes the best container for the food. But you may wrap the food in wet leaves or vegetables, or use heavy aluminum foil or cooking bags. If a Dutch oven is not used in the hole, place meat in first, then vegetables, then leaves, then coals and rocks, then soil to cover.

Barbecuing on a spit outdoors is much different than doing it electrically back home. But it's more fun. Take time for turning and basting while you're sitting around the fire, chatting about the events of the day.

For this you also dig a pit, and build a good hardwood fire in it. It's good to have another fire nearby with hot coals so you can add them periodically to keep the fire hot.

Place the meat on the spit and fasten it firmly in place so that it will turn with the stick and cook evenly. When barbecuing a chicken, select a broiler about two pounds in weight. Then you can put several on one spit for more people (1 chicken serves 2—4 people). Clean the bird well and insert spit firmly from tail to neck. Protect wings and legs from burning by pinning them close to the body with wooden slivers. Rotate the spit slowly over the coals, baste every ten minutes with melted butter, bacon grease, or shortening. Apply with swab made from cloth tied around end of stick.

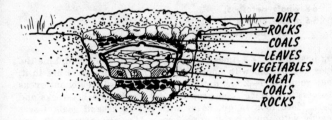

FIG. 32
Pit Barbecue

FIG. 33
Spit Barbecue

Have handle of the spit long enough so that you can stay well back from the fire. Place notches at varying heights for adjusting the spit to the proper distance from the heat. You can use a peeled green stick for a spit, or bring a metal rod from home. Roast of beef, pork, or ducks and turkey, or small game may be cooked in this manner.

Camp cooking possibilities with a spit are limited, of course, and most cooking of this type requires more time than most campers want to devote to a meal preparation.

Another variation of cooking on a spit is to cook at the side of a fire with a drip pan underneath. Some campers prefer this method. To do this, suspend the meat by a cord or wire from a lug pole five to six feet above the ground and on the leeward side of the fire. Insert a flat piece of wood or flattened No. 10 tin can about half way down the string. Even on a rather still day, the can will catch enough breeze to keep the meat turning automatically so that it cooks evenly. Prepare the chicken as described above and reverse the lug pole and meat periodically to cook both sides. Set a pan under the meat to catch the drippings, and baste it every 10-15 minutes. A reflector wall on the leeward (with the wind) side makes the cooking faster (See Fig. 21).

Fish Cookery

In this short space, it would be impossible to give you all the good ideas on fish cookery. There are already on the market many fine books that deal solely with the preparation and cooking of fish.

If you're game to do the fishing, then I'll just say a word about cleaning and preparing them.

Fish is one of the most nutritious foods that you could select, low in fat, high in protein. There must be some reason why Weight Watchers require it so often in their diet.

Now I don't claim to be the world's best fish cleaner, in fact I've done it only a few times. But after the first time, it didn't seem so hard after all.

Cleaning Fish

Keep fish as dry and cool as possible. Clean and cook soon after catching. Start by taking a sharp knife and cutting off the head (optional). Next, slit it from top to bottom on belly side, remove entrails. Then cut off the gills. The tail cooks crisp and can be removed better later to conserve more meat. Then wash fish inside and out, and dry.

To filet fish, clean first. Then make longitudinal cut down back side, separate from bones with a slice of the knife, without entering body cavity.

If you wish to remove the skin, lay the filet on the edge of a flat surface, skin side down. Beginning at the tail end, work the knife between skin and flesh. Holding this end of skin, slice forward with knife blade flat against the inside of the skin. The filet can be sliced off, leaving no flesh on the skin and no skin on the filet. If fish are to be fileted, it is unnecessary to scale them.

The best way to pack dry fish is in plastic bags, with as little air as possible. This way it can be carried in a portable cooler without getting wet and spreading the fishy odor to other foods. If you have some cornmeal, roll the fish filets in it, coating liberally, before packing them away. It helps to keep them dry and in cold weather they will need little refrigeration for a day or two.

Fish, when properly fried, are delicious, but too many cooks stop there. This is unfortunate, because no food can be cooked in as many different ways as fish. One can bake them, boil them, broil them, or fry them. They can be filled with stuffings, marinated or served with tasty sauces. One can make them into fish cakes or fish balls. And one can use them in a variety of soups, chowders, and stews.

The following recipes are but a few that are good to use for camp cookery.

Planked Broiled Fish

Find a splinter-free, hardwood board of suitable size. You may use a short split log also. Be sure you have removed the head and scales from a large fish and scaled it. Then split it down the back, leaving the belly skin intact. Remove entrails and dark material under backbone. Wash and wipe dry. After cleaning board or plank, use small tacks or nails to put the fish, skin side down, on the wood. Prop the fish near the fire, as shown in the illustration (See Fig. 34). While it is cooking, brush it with bacon grease or barbecue sauce. You may have to adjust the plank to be sure the fish broils evenly at the proper heat.

When the fish flakes from the skin, add salt and pepper, and serve it from the plank, allowing most of the skin to remain sticking to the plank. Cook from 20—30 minutes depending on heat and size of fish.

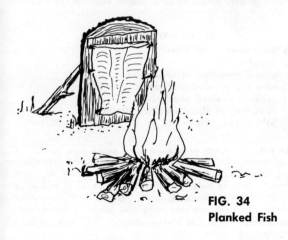

FIG. 34
Planked Fish

FOIL BAKED FISH CHUNKS

    2 fish chunks, about ¾ pound each
    1 tomato, sliced
    1 onion, sliced
    2 T. butter or margarine
    4 T. water
      Salt, pepper

Place each fish chunk on a square of heavy-duty aluminum foil.
Top each with half the tomato, onion and butter, pour water over
it, season to taste. Fold each square of foil into a package, sealing
well. Lay on grate 4 inches above medium coals. Turn once, cooking a total of 15-20 minutes. Packages can be cooked directly
on top of the coals if desired.

FISH BALLS

    1 c. cooked fish, flaked
    1 c. mashed potatoes (instant or leftover)
      May add cooked peas as well
    1 egg, well beaten
    1 tsp. melted butter
      Salt, pepper
    2 c. hot bacon fat or cooking oil

Combine all ingredients except fat. Drop by teaspoon into hot,
deep fat, and fry until golden brown. Drain on paper towels and
serve while very hot, with catsup or lemon wedges.

FISH CHOWDER

    1-1½ lbs. boneless fish filets
       ¾ c. water
         Liquid from can of vegetables
       2 cans golden mushroom soup
       1 16-oz. can mixed vegetables
       1 16-oz. can of sliced potatoes, drained
         Salt, pepper, onion salt

Put fish in pot, add water and liquid from vegetables, cover and
bring to a simmer. Continue to cook just until the fish flakes
(very short time). Remove fish with slotted spoon and set aside.
Add mushroom soup to water in which fish was cooked and bring
to a simmer, stirring constantly until smooth. Add vegetables
and potatoes. Continue cooking over low coals, stirring until
vegetables are hot. Add salt and seasonings. Add fish, as soon
as heated through, serve.

PAN FISH FRIED IN BATTER

2-4 medium pan fish, freshwater or saltwater
1 egg, lightly beaten
¼ c. milk
½ c. toasted bread crumbs, cracker crumbs, cornmeal
2-4 T. cooking oil
Salt, pepper
Lemon wedges

Combine egg and milk or canned milk, dip pan fish in the mixture, then coat with crumbs and lay on a clean, flat surface to dry 3—5 minutes. Heat oil in large skillet to sizzling hot. Add fish, fry until golden brown on both sides. Salt and pepper and serve with lemon wedges.

CHARCOAL BROILED CAMP TROUT

6 medium sized fresh-caught rainbow trout, dressed
Salt, pepper
2 T. butter or margarine
Lemon wedges

Arrange fish in long-handled hinged grill and broil about 4 inches above burned down cooking coals. Cook about 4—6 minutes to a side or until fish flakes easily when gently probed with the tines of a fork. Serve. Let each season his own.

FRIED THIN FILETS

6-8 filets
1 c. flour
½ tsp. salt
⅛ tsp. pepper
3 T. olive oil
3 T. butter or margarine
Juice of 1 lemon

Mix flour, salt, pepper, and toss filets in it to coat thoroughly. Fry slowly in mixture of oil and butter until golden brown. Transfer to platter. Add lemon juice to the fat, stir, pour over fish.

Fat for frying should be very hot but not smoking. A good test is to have several bread crumbs handy. When the fat seems about right, drop a crumb in it. If crumb swims and bubbles, it's time to put fish in. Don't put all the fish in at once, because it reduces the temperature. Add one piece at a time. Be sure pieces keep on bubbling vigorously while cooking.

When the fish is a golden brown on one side, turn it over to get the other side brown. Overcooking makes it dry and tough. Then dry on absorbent towels, season, and dig in!

SKILLET SALMON SUPPER
(Serves 6-8)

    6 slices bacon
    1/3 c. chopped onion or 2 T. instant minced onion
    1 pkg. au gratin potato mix
    1 tsp. salt
    1/2 tsp. thyme
    Dash pepper
    2 c. water
    1 1/2 c. milk
    1 can whole kernel corn, drained
    2 c. cooked flaked salmon or tuna (2 cans)

In large fry pan or Dutch oven, fry bacon until crisp; set aside. To bacon drippings, add remaining ingredients except salmon; mix well. Cover and simmer about 15 minutes until potatoes are tender. Add salmon; heat through.

HOMEMADE TARTAR SAUCE

Tartar sauce goes with fried fish as well as ham goes with eggs. If you didn't bring any to camp, make your own with a few handy ingredients.

    1 c. mayonnaise
    2 T. chopped dill pickle
    2 T. chopped onion (or instant minced)
    2 T. finely chopped parsley
    Lemon juice

Mix together. If no dill pickle, any kind of pickle will do, or chopped olives, or pickle relish.

HUSH PUPPIES

A great side dish for fish are hush puppies. They are a Southern cornmeal-based fritter, which should be fried in the fat the fish are fried in, to give them real flavor. Here's one simple recipe.

    2 c. cornmeal
    1 c. flour
    1/2 tsp. salt
    2 tsp. baking powder
    1 large onion, chopped fine
    4 T. ham or bacon fat

Combine all ingredients and work in enough water to make a stiff dough. Roll into small balls or into lengths about half the size of your finger. Fry in the fat with the fish until they are golden brown. Drain on absorbent paper and serve hot with the fish.

FISH STEW

2-3 lbs. fish filets, cut in small cubes
½ c. flour
½ c. olive oil
1 onion, chopped (or minced onion)
2 small red or 1 green pepper, chopped
1 T. parsley flakes
1 clove garlic, minced
1 can Italian tomato sauce
⅓ c. water

Put the fish and flour in a paper bag and shake to coat fish with flour. Put the oil in a skillet, add the fish, onion, peppers, parsley, and garlic. Saute these until the fish is lightly browned. Then add the tomato sauce and water. Season with salt and pepper. Cover and cook slowly over medium coals for 30 minutes. Add a little water to thin the stew.

CHEESE STUFFED FISH
(Serves 5)

½ c. sliced fresh mushrooms
¼ c. chopped green onion
2 T. Parmesan cheese
2 lbs. whole fish (any kind of lean fish can be used)

Spoon onion, mushrooms and cheese into cavity of fish as stuffing. Season with salt and pepper. Secure with toothpicks or metal nails (as used on stuffed turkey). Broil or grill over hot coals about 8 minutes each side until fish flakes. To prepare in skillet, stuff fish and dip in flour. Fry in small amount of hot fat.

Game Meat Cookery

The average hunter today has two strikes against him before he ever gets to cook. First, he must catch a good animal, then he must dress it properly and get it under refrigeration quickly.

Keep game meat cool at all times and tenderize by hanging for a while as sides of beef are treated. Then cook properly, and marinate if the animal is older.

Bear meat can be excellent when properly prepared.

A young one tastes better than pork, many will testify. And bear meat should be prepared like pork. Always remove the fat because the gamy flavor comes from it.

BEAR STEAK CASSEROLE

Marinate the steak overnight; wipe it dry, and cut it into 2 inch squares. Roll each in seasoned flour, fry in greased skillet until well browned. Transfer meat to a Dutch oven or large pot, pour over it the following:

    ½ c. water
    ½ t. ground bay leaves
    1 onion, chopped
      Dash of garlic salt and pepper

Cover the casserole and bake for several hours in a pit or for 1½ hours in medium coals.

DEER CHOPS

Only marinate if tough. Afterwards, place in pan with seasonings, sprinkle with tenderizer and olive oil. Put in cooler for a few hours, roll in crumbs or flour before frying. Don't overcook!

The liver of the animal may be cooked much like you fix liver any other way. Saute onions with it.

SKILLET STEW

    2 lbs. venison, large cubes
    ½ c. flour and seasonings
    5 T. olive oil or cooking oil
    1 onion, chopped fine
    2 cloves garlic
    2 T. parsley flakes

Roll meat in flour, sear in oil, fry the other ingredients in the skillet with the meat. Be sure the garlic does not burn, remove it. Add 1 c. water. Cover skillet tightly and allow meat to simmer for 1 hour until meat is tender. Add more water if necessary. Add salt and pepper to taste, with a pinch of oregano. When meat is tender, stir in 2 T. tomato paste until blended (may substitute tomatoes or catsup). Serve over rice, noodles, or with mashed potatoes.

More people eat rabbit than any other game. Rabbits have white meat that closely resembles chicken. When the rabbit has been skinned and cleaned, remove and divide both hindquarters and forequarters. Once dressed they are ready to cook.

BAKED RABBIT

Clean, cut in halves. Place in large skillet, spread lavishly with butter or margarine, cover, bake in very hot oven for an hour, or in hot coals for 1½ hrs. Baste several times.

In cooking rabbit, marinades and high seasonings are not recommended. They interfere with the fine flavor of the meat. Use lots of butter, rather than cooking oils. Rabbit is a lean meat, which needs the addition of butter.

FRIED RABBIT

       2 young rabbits
       2 egg yolks, beaten
       3 c. milk
    1¼ c. flour
       1 tsp. salt
    ½ c. butter
       2 T. currant or grape jelly
       1 T. minced parsley

Wash dressed rabbits in cold water, dry, cut in serving size pieces. Combine eggs and milk, gradually add 1 c. flour and salt, beat until batter is smooth. Dip meat in batter, and fry in butter until golden brown. Move to medium coals, cover and cook 30—40 minutes. Remove when done to warm plate, use remaining flour to put in skillet with fat. Add 2 c. milk to mixture, stirring constantly to make gravy. Pour over rabbit pieces, garnish with jelly and parsley.

STEWED SQUIRREL

       2 or more squirrels, quartered
    ½ c. flour
    ½ tsp. salt
       Dash of pepper
       4 T. butter or margarine

Wash squirrels; wipe dry and coat thoroughly with the seasoned flour. Fry in butter, turning until all sides are light brown. Fry in medium coals so butter does not burn. Remove meat from skillet. Add flour to butter in skillet gradually, stirring constantly. After a paste is made, stir in water gradually to make a thin gravy. Return the meat to the gravy, cover and cook over low to medium coals for one hour or until tender. Add water as needed, and a bay leaf or other spices for flavor.

This recipe can be used for rabbits, game birds, or other game. Groundhog, or woodchuck, tastes about the same as squirrel. After dressing properly, it can be cooked the same way as has been described for rabbits or squirrels.

111

FRIED SQUIRREL

1 squirrel
1 T. salt
1 egg
1 T. milk
½ c. dried bread crumbs
2 T. cooking oil
Salt, pepper

Cut into serving pieces, soak in cold, salted water for one hour, batter, then roll in seasoned crumbs. Melt oil in skillet, when hot, fry squirrel meat, turning until golden brown. Move to medium coals, remove meat from skillet and drain on paper towels.

MARINADE

You probably have your own special marinade for any game meat, but for those of you who don't remember, most marinades are made up of wine vinegar and spices. Onions erase the gamy taste and add flavor. Most game meat should be fully covered and marinated for about 24 hours or overnight. Marinade may be reused once or twice. Here is a suggested recipe:

Juice of 1 lemon
½ c. tarragon wine vinegar
2 onions, sliced
1 tsp. chili powder
½ c. water
2 tsp. salt
2 bay leaves
¼ tsp. black pepper
½ c. tomato catsup
1 garlic clove, crushed

Game Birds

Game birds take a slightly different treatment than the domestic kind. Pheasants, quail, and grouse have very little body fat and must be cooked in butter, or bacon fat. Young birds are best and can be prepared by frying or barbecuing, while older birds are tough and should be used only in stews and casseroles.

All birds should be plucked and dressed the same day they are shot. Then they should be kept in a cooler for several days or frozen for longer keeping.

The birds should be plucked at once, because quill feathers stiffen into the skin when birds have been cooled. This is when you want to leave the skin in tact. Of course, to skin it would be easier. First, chop off the wings close to the body. Their meat is too tough and there is too little. Remove the legs at the knees. Slit skin under the tail and skin back over the breast and up the body toward the neck. Break breast away from the back. The breast is the best part of most game birds.

To hasten plucking, dip the bird in hot paraffin and boiling water. If any fuzz remains, use Sterno canned heat to singe it off. Clean out insides, put in onion slices, which will be removed before cooking. These remove the gamy taste. Then refrigerate. When ready to cook, especially ducks, place in cold salt water overnight. This removes strong flavors and blood clots.

When ducks are cooked over the open fire, they should not be cooked directly over the coals, because the dripping and burning fat will cause too much flare-up. Set a foil pan under the bird to catch the drippings, after pushing the coals back where dripping fat will not affect them (See Fig. 27).

Listed below are a few recipes. Most of them can apply to all types of game birds.

BAKED DUCK WITH BARBECUE SAUCE

 2 ducks
 1 c. wine vinegar
   Salt, pepper
 ½ c. flour
 ½ c. bacon or other fat

Skin ducks, cut into serving size pieces. Cover pieces with water, add vinegar. Let stand for 3 hours or overnight. Drain and dry pieces. Roll each in seasoned flour. Brown in hot fat. Remove fat from skillet, pour your favorite barbecue sauce over meat. You can use a commercially prepared sauce. You may add onion, garlic and celery to this. Cover skillet and bake over medium coals for 1—2 hrs. Do not overcook because meat will become dry and crumbly.

DUCKS IN FOIL

With onion left in body cavity, tie legs and wings and tuck several strips of bacon in, or wrap breast with bacon. Wrap in heavy-duty foil twice. Put right in coals or on grid over the coals. Cook for one hour.

DUCK ON A SPIT

After dressing and soaking bird, tie legs and wings close to body. Balance duck on spit. Put foil pan underneath. As the duck turns on the spit, it will baste itself but basting with a marinade sauce helps the flavor.

DUCK MARINADE SAUCE

¼ c. vinegar
¼ c. salad oil
2 tsp. salt
¼ tsp. dry mustard
½ garlic clove, crushed
Dash of herbs, nutmeg, clove

Can be used for marinade or basting.

In the woods, a one-inch thick, green, peeled, straight sapling, pointed at the end, will serve as a spit. It can be positioned at right distance over the coals and turned by hand. You may wrap the spitted bird in foil to retain the juices and to prevent ashes from getting on the meat. But if you prefer a slightly smoky flavor, do not use foil.

Since geese are big birds, they are usually roasted. Hunters who want a quick meal like to fry the breasts. Use this recipe:

FRIED GOOSE BREASTS

1 pair (or more) of goose breasts
¼ c. flour
Salt, pepper
¼ c. bacon fat
Water or milk

Skin the goose and slice out the whole breasts. Slice about ¼ inch thick, across the grain. Dredge in seasoned flour, and pound, to tenderize. Fry in hot fat for one minute on each side. Remove the meat from the pan and stir in 1 T. flour for each 1 T. fat remaining. When smooth, stir in water or milk to make gravy of the right consistency. Add salt, pepper, or other condiments to the gravy, and pour it over fried goose breasts. Continue to cook, covered, for 30 minutes or until tender.

Geese can be cooked on a spit oven, an open fire, in a Dutch oven, in coals in the ground, or wrapped securely in aluminum foil and cooked as ducks.

Pheasants can be cooked exactly as you cook chicken. But since it is a wild bird, a few more ingredients have been added to the recipes for more outdoor flavor.

PHEASANT IN MUSHROOM SAUCE

1 dressed pheasant
½ c. flour
½ tsp. salt
¼ tsp. pepper
½ tsp. paprika
½ c. shortening or oil
1 can mushroom soup and ¼ c. milk

Cut the pheasant in serving size pieces. Put in paper bag with next four ingredients. Shake to coat pieces with flour. Put oil in skillet until very hot, fry meat in oil until brown. Mix soup and milk together, pour over meat and continue cooking, covered, over medium coals for 30 minutes or until tender. Then remove and make gravy of drippings (add 1 tsp. flour and ½ c. milk).

This same recipe can be done in a Dutch oven, in the coals, or in a big pot over the fire. You might want to add a small can of drained green peas a few minutes before the bird is done.

PHEASANT IN FOIL

2 pheasant breasts
4 pineapple rings
4 T. cooking sherry

Take a square pan or skillet and lay the pineapple rings in it. Season the breast and lay them over the pineapple. Add the cooking sherry. Crimp a large doubled sheet of heavy-duty aluminum foil over the skillet so steam cannot escape. Bake on the grill over medium coals for an hour.

For cooking right in the foil, take a large, heavy square; place in one breast, 2 pineapple rings, and 2 T. cooking sherry. Wrap up securely. Place in coals for an hour, turning every 15 minutes.

Wild Turkey, Camp Style

Use aluminum foil, a heavy skillet with a lid, or a Dutch oven. Cut up the bird like a chicken. Using a paper bag, coat in seasoned flour. Place the pieces on a large, doubled square of heavy-duty tin foil (or in the pan or oven) and add 4 T. butter. Fold up the edges of the foil to make a platter, and pour over the turkey ½ c. cooking sherry. Fold the foil to make a tight package and put an outer wrapping around this, so no juices can leak out. Put the package on the grill or on hot coals. Cooking time will vary from 1 to 1½ hours, depending on the heat of the coals and the size of the bird. Turn foil package every 15 minutes.

Another method is to cut up the turkey and boil the bony parts in a little water, with seasoning and a bay leaf. Remove the meat from the bones and add it to the meat that has been cooked in the foil. Cook some Rice-a-Roni to go with it, or using stock from cooking bones, make a nice bowl of Minute Rice. Serve meat and rice together.

This chapter contains only the basic information needed to prepare and serve game meat and poultry. Before hunting, it would be well to check the recipes included to be sure to take all the needed ingredients for cooking the game you are seeking.

Trail Traveler Tips

This little book is excellent for the backpacker. It contains all the recipes and cooking ideas he would need. And it fits neatly in a little space in his pack. Many recipes especially for backpackers are included in the One-Pot Meal section. And, of course, most of the time he will cook right on the grill or in a skillet (look to those sections as well). But a few extra tips are contained here.

Check whether you will need to carry water or not. Check with your nearest camping outfitters for the latest in freeze-dried foods. They are delicious and of such great variety. The extra expense is worth it if you must travel light.

Dehydrated foods used to be avoided like poison,

because they tasted so awful. But things have changed. Check your grocer's shelves for soups, stews, juices, puddings, hot cereal, rice dishes, and many, many more.

The easiest foods to carry are those on which temperature has little effect—dried peas, beans, rice, cereal, cake mixes, macaroni, cheese, and candies. But keep them tightly sealed in high humidity areas.

Don't overlook the possibility of locating wild foods in the woods. But be knowledgeable before you start to devour such. Take along a cookbook for preparing natural foods. There are many out now, some in paperback.

Concentrate on a high ratio of nourishment to weight and bulk in the foodstuff you carry. Don't pack food that you've never tried before; do your experimenting ahead of time.

We said this before, but it bears repeating. Repack foods in usable pliable containers. Glass bottles break. Would you believe salad oil in the sleeping bag? Transfer liquids into leakproof plastic bottles; put bulk items (flour, sugar, powdered milk) into plastic bags; semi-solids (peanut butter, jam) in washable, plastic squeeze tubes.

You save a lot of space and rubbish too, if you repack cereal and other boxed foods. Eggs are best broken into a thermos; no shells, no worry about breakage and spoilage. Canned goods add weight, but a few small ones may be just the thing for a tasty meal. Don't forget the spices and condiments!

Include some high energy foods for quick nourishment. Health food stores and camp outfitters carry such things as tropical chocolate, sucrose drops, pemmican, sesame bars, trail biscuits, and bacon bars. These are great for your sagging body and drooping spirits. If you don't make it to one of these stores, include some hard candy for energy and some beef jerky for protein. It'll do wonders for you on the trail, especially if it's your first try at trail traveling.

Trip Counselor's Menus

Every counselor who takes a group of kids on a camp-out for several days has the task of making out menus for the days on the trail. And each counselor would like to get his hands on some menus that all the kids will like and that are easy to fix. Well, here they are: All you have to do is copy them out for the cook, putting down exact amounts according to the size of your group. All recipes are to be found in this book, so put it in your pocket when you take off on your trip.

MEAL	MARKET LIST
Breakfast	
Fresh quartered oranges	Fresh oranges (1 each) or
Pancakes	canned orange slices (⅓ can)
Bacon	Instant pancake mix
Milk, cocoa, coffee	Syrup
	Butter or margarine
	Bacon (1 strip each)
	Instant chocolate mix (1 cup each)
	Powdered milk
	Instant coffee (adults only)
Lunch	
Grilled cheese sandwiches	Cheese slices (1 each)
Stuffed celery	Bread (2 slices each)
Carrot sticks	Margarine
Apple, cookies	Celery, carrots
Lemonade	Peanut butter
	Apples (1 ea.)
	Cookies (box)
	Instant Lemonade
Dinner	
Golden grilled fish	Fresh or frozen fish (1 filet ea.)
Golden corn	Cooking oil
Potato sticks	Canned, fresh, or frozen corn
Doughboys, butter	(½ c. ea.)
Instant lemon pudding	Potato sticks (large can)
with berries	Prepared biscuit mix
Milk, coffee	Powdered milk (reconstituted)

MEAL	MARKET LIST
	Margarine or butter, jelly
	Instant lemon pudding
	Fresh or frozen berries
	Lemon wedges (opt.)
	Instant coffee

Breakfast

Grape juice	Powdered grape drink
Scrambled eggs/Bacos	Eggs (1-2 per person)
Toast	Jar of Bacos
Milk, cocoa, coffee	Bread (1-2 slices each)
	Margarine, jelly
	Powdered milk
	Instant chocolate mix
	Instant coffee
	Sugar and cream (opt.)
	Salt, pepper

Lunch

Mini pizzaburgers	English muffins or hamburger buns
Lemonade	Spaghetti sauce
Peaches	Ground beef, cooked and drained
Cookies	Mozzarella cheese
	Oregano
	Instant lemonade mix
	Canned or freeze-dried peaches
	Box of cookies, or slice refrigerated cookies and bake in reflector oven

Dinner

Tin foil dinner	Potatoes, carrots, onions (all sliced thin, in separate bowls)
Tossed salad	Hamburger patty (1 each)
Bread, butter	Heavy-duty aluminum foil (2 squares each)
Banana boats	Butter or margarine
Milk, coffee	Salt, pepper
	Lettuce, tart dressing
	Bananas (1 each)
	Plain chocolate bars (1 each)
	Miniature marshmallows

MEAL	MARKET LIST
	Bread or quick-baked rolls
	Milk
	Instant coffee

Breakfast

Grapefruit drink	Powdered grapefruit drink
Hot cereal	Prepackaged hot cereal
Milk, sugar	Powdered milk (reconstituted)
Cinnamon toast	Sugar and cinnamon mixed
Milk, coffee	Bread
	Butter or margarine
	Instant coffee
	Powdered cream (opt.)

Lunch

Dilly Dogs	Hot dogs (1-2 each)
Potato chips	Cheese slices
Carrot, celery sticks	Bacon (1 slice each)
Instant butterscotch pudding	Toothpicks or use wood slivers
and nuts	Hot dog buns
Milk	Catsup, mustard, relish
	Canned potato chips
	Carrots, celery (cut in strips)
	Instant butterscotch
	pudding/walnuts
	Milk

Dinner

Chicken on a Spit	Whole dressed chicken (1 per 5)
Mashed potatoes	Instant mashed potatoes
Freeze-dried peas	Freeze-dried peas (reconstituted)
Bread Twister	Powdered milk (reconstituted)
Butter, jelly	Prepared biscuit mix
Milk/coffee	Butter or margarine, jelly
Chocolate pie	Instant coffee
	Graham cracker crumbs
	Sugar
	Instant chocolate pie mix

Breakfast

Apple juice	Powdered apple cider mix
French toast	Eggs
Butter, syrup	Powdered milk (reconstituted)
Sausage	Salt, pepper
Milk, coffee	Day-old bread or rolls

MEAL	MARKET LIST

	Sausage links, or bulk
	Instant coffee
	Sugar (opt.)
	Butter or margarine
	Syrup

Lunch
Angels on Horseback
Chicken soup
Walking salad
Frosted cookies
Cold strawberry drink

Bacon slices (1 each)
Hamburger buns
Lettuce
Cheese chunks
Instant chicken soup mix
Apples (1 each)
Raisin or peanut butter
Day-old cookies or crackers
Prepared canned frosting
Instant powdered drink mix

Dinner
Skillet Salmon Supper
Cucumbers/onion salad
Tart dressing such as Italian
Bread, butter
Coconut Snackin' cake
Milk, coffee, tea

Salmon or tuna
Bacon
Minced onion
Au gratin potato mix
Canned corn
Milk (real or powdered)
Salt, pepper
Cucumbers, onions
Tart dressing (buy or make)
Bread, butter
Instant coconut cake
Instant coffee
Instant tea

Breakfast
Orange juice
Wrapped fish filets
Scrambled eggs
Toast
Milk, coffee

Powdered orange juice mix
Fish filets (1-2 each)
Bacon slices (wrap around fish)
Eggs
Bread, butter, jelly
Powdered milk (reconstituted)
Instant coffee
Powdered cream, sugar (opt.)
Salt, pepper

MEAL	MARKET LIST

Lunch

Peanut butter, bacon and
banana sandwich
Vegetable soup
Pudding parfait
Cold cherry drink

Peanut butter
Bacon bits (in jar or fried fresh)
Bananas
Bread (2 slices each)
Instant soup mix
Crackers
Instant butterscotch pudding
  mix
Powdered milk (reconstituted)
Chocolate ice cream topping
Nuts or crisp cereal
Powdered drink mix

Dinner

Meat Turnover
  (reflector oven)
Corn on the cob
Leafy salad
Tart dressing such as
  blue cheese
Peachy pudding dessert
Milk, coffee

Prepared biscuit mix
Milk (for biscuits, pudding,
  drink)
Margarine
Cooked or canned meat
Pickle relish or chili sauce
Fresh corn (cooked in coals)
Tossed lettuce greens
Radish or celery (salad)
Tart salad dressing (buy or
  make)
Peaches (fresh or canned)
Honey
Instant vanilla pudding
Instant coffee
Powdered cream, sugar (opt.)
Seasonings

123

125